Artwork © María Udriot

Structural Change, Openness and Development in the Argentine Economy

First published in 1991, *Structural Change, Openness and Development in the Argentine Economy* is a model-based study that analyzes the impact of global economic reconfiguration at the time on Argentina's economy. The book investigates strategic adjustments necessary to navigate the challenges posed by these changes.

It delves into the root causes of Argentina's economic stagnation and provides a comprehensive analysis of how openness – through trade liberalization, foreign investment, and integration into global markets – shaped the country's economic development. The study highlights both the challenges and opportunities arising from these transformations, offering valuable insights into policy strategies aimed at fostering sustainable growth.

Structural Change, Openness and Development in the Argentine Economy is an essential resource for students and researchers interested in Latin American economies and the effects of globalization on developing nations.

Structural Change, Openness and Development in the Argentine Economy

Jorge Buzaglo

Routledge
Taylor & Francis Group

First published in 1991
by Avebury

This edition first published in 2026 by Routledge
4 Park Square, Milton Park, Abingdon, Oxon, OX14 4RN

and by Routledge
605 Third Avenue, New York, NY 10158

Routledge is an imprint of the Taylor & Francis Group, an informa business

Publisher's Note
The publisher has gone to great lengths to ensure the quality of this reprint but points out that some imperfections in the original copies may be apparent.

Disclaimer
The publisher has made every effort to trace copyright holders and welcomes correspondence from those they have been unable to contact.
For Product Safety Concerns and Information please contact our EU representative GPSR@taylorandfrancis.com. Taylor & Francis Verlag GmbH, Kaufingerstraße 24, 80331 München, Germany.

A Library of Congress record exists under LCCN: 91044632

ISBN: 978-1-041-17088-4 (hbk)
ISBN: 978-1-003-68791-7 (ebk)
ISBN: 978-1-041-17095-2 (pbk)

Book DOI 10.4324/9781003687917

Structural Change, Openness and Development in the Argentine Economy

JORGE BUZAGLO

Department of Economics
University of Stockholm

Avebury

Aldershot · Brookfield USA · Hong Kong · Singapore · Sydney

First published in Spanish 1989, revised English edition 1991

Published by
Avebury
Academic Publishing Group
Gower House
Croft Road
Aldershot
Hants GU11 3HR
England

Gower Publishing Company
Old Post Road
Brookfield
Vermont 05036
USA

A CIP catalogue record for this book is available from the British Library and the US Library of Congress.

ISBN 1 85628 251 1

Printed in Great Britain by
Athenaeum Press Ltd, Newcastle upon Tyne.

Contents

Acknowledgments

This study could not have been performed without the goodwill, talent and patience of many people. I would first like to mention Irene Loiseau, who collaborated on implementing the model on which this work is based, and in formulating and executing the simulation and optimization experiments. Eleonora Poyard, Isabel Méndez and María Teresa Carlini also contributed to this part of the work.

The process of compiling the detailed numerical representation of the Argentine economy was facilitated by the Argentine Institute of Statistics (INDEC), with particular help from Luis Beccaria and Víctor Beker, as well as from Carlos Alonso, who provided invaluable guidance with the intricate data labyrinths. I am indebted to almost all units of the INDEC for their support and would like to mention the authors of the estimation of the expenditure system in the model – Pablo Lucci, Humberto Marino and Laura Scipioni. Andrea Bentolila also assisted me in this part of the work.

I am grateful for help and hospitality at the Institute of Economic Research, University of Buenos Aires, particularly from Julio H. G. Olivera and Alejandro Moledo. Hugo Scolnik and participants of his seminar at the Facultad de Ciencias Exactas, University of Buenos Aires, also contributed to clarifying my ideas. I am indebted to Adolfo Canitrot, Daniel Heymann,

Edgardo Lifschitz, Angel Peña, Alejandro Rausch, Jorge Schvarzer and Otilia Vainstok for comments and suggestions.

As a researcher at the Department of Economics at the University of Stockholm, I benefited from exposure to some dose of scientific radiation. I would also like to thank the Institute of Latin American Studies, the Department of Physics and the Library of that university for their support. At the Department of Economics, University of Gothenburg, I received useful comments and suggestions, in particular from Arne Bigsten, Renato Aguilar and Mario Zejan. Parts of the work were discussed at the Eighth Nordic Research Conference on Latin America and at the Ninth International Conference on Input-Output Techniques.

I am indebted to Julie Sundqvist for her help in editing the English text. I also thank Bo Kåwe for assistance with the word processing and my friend Carlos Narvaja for his help with the graphics.

I am also most grateful to Kajsa Buzaglo Olofsgård, and to Clara, my mother, for their loving inspiration and support.

Last but not least, I would like to join the Spanish novelist in thanking 'my enemies, who have helped me so much'.

This work benefited from financial support from the Swedish Agency for Research Cooperation with Developing Countries and the United Nations Development Programme.

My gratitude — *cela va sans dire* — does not by any means implicate the above persons and institutions in the contents of this work, for which I am exclusively responsible.

J.B.

1 Introduction

Along with progressive reconstitution of civil society and political democracy, a protracted period of profound dissension and harsh controversy seems to be coming to an end in Argentina. During this critical period, the economic and social landscape of the country has changed dramatically.

These changes are also part of an ongoing process of crisis and transformation in the international economic system. Underlying this process are shocks to production systems from powerful waves of technical innovations, and the stress and strain of adjusting lagging social regulatory institutions to rapid technological advances. The contemporary technological revolution has not only globalized technical and production systems, but also eroded national governing systems. A free global market has displaced regulated national markets. Although free and not subject to control, the global market is not a purely competitive market; rather it conforms to an oligopoly, whose evolution is marked by conflict or cooperation. The type of interaction which tends to dominate determines the configuration of the evolving international scene.

In the conflict case, the tendency is towards dislocation. Different coalitions tend to prevail throughout a fragmented global system. Economies introvert; productive systems tend to recede into nation-states. Democratic governing systems tend to direct reallocation towards increased welfare, whereas autocratic systems tend to concentrate on national strength.

In the cooperation case, the tendency is towards increasing global integration and openness. The democratic form represents a historical mutation, with a surge of global governance guided by regulation principles based on justice and rationality. The nondemocratic, collusive form, based exclusively on the requirements of the techno-productive system, is unstable, and tends to drift towards the democratic global *polis*, or towards some form of fragmentation. But even fragmentation could be regarded as a transient interruption in the basic trend towards the global *polis*.

What are the effects of these reconfigurations of the global scene on an economy such as Argentina's? What are the best strategic adjustments to the conditions created by these changes?

These are the main concerns of our study. The inquiry is conducted by means of a model of the Argentine economy. The model may be likened to a sonde, used to explore alternative configuration scenarios for the economy. The guiding principles are simplicity and consistency, given the expected detail and scope of the inquiry. The analysis of dynamic adjustment of the economy to increased openness, or the implications of establishing a self-sufficient economy, call for a multisectoral model. In order to study effects on the level and distribution of income, different income classes are allowed for. Structural policy instruments which influence the pattern of development are also included.

First, the model is applied to explore the recent past. During this period, the Argentine economy stagnated. The model suggests explanatory factors, i.e., capital outflows and inefficiency in the use of productive capacities. The immediate causes of Argentine economic stagnation seem to reside in very large capital outflows, much larger than those indicated by national account statistics, and in very low investment efficiency. Underlying these factors are the global economic crisis and its effects (high interest rates, uncertainty, etc.), amplified internally by weakened regulatory mechanisms and fragile productive structures.

The model is then applied to explore several possible futures for the Argentine economy. Status quo in the context of irresolvability of global tensions, with high interest rates, uncertainties about market values and regulatory norms, etc., implies persistence of the present stagnating regime. Under conditions of economic morass, the Argentine economy exhibits extreme rigidity. External debt moratorium, for instance, does not succeed in mitigating stagnation. Moreover, attempts to 'close' the economy and become self-sufficient seem doomed to failure; it does not seem possible to change output composition, trade patterns or the degree of openness of the economy to any noticeable extent.

Resolution of existing tensions results in new evolutionary regimes. By either fragmentation or integration, the tensions which affect the functioning of the world economy are released. In a framework of either reregulation and control, or global openness and articulation, investment activity regains effectiveness and momentum.

The most elementary form of fragmentation is a simple nationalistic reaction. Debt servicing is suspended and the economy is closed. The objectives are autonomy and maximal self-sufficiency in production. The model solution for these objectives gives an optimal investment plan which attains a high level of fulfilment. It does not seem possible, however, to close the economy totally within the planning horizon (ten years).

Another form of fragmentation is a more elaborated response, where autonomy and self-sufficiency are supplemented by increased equality in distribution. The redistributive strategy suggests a sociopolitical environment of democratization. The growth effects of a redistribution strategy do not seem to be negative in the Argentine case. Our examination indicates a positive impact on welfare. The resulting optimal investment plan, with slightly different sectoral priorities than in the nondistribution case, obtains a high level of fulfilment.

We then turn to the cases of global integration and openness. They imply a systemic mutation, with a surge of global regulatory norms and institutions and an environment of increased symmetry and transparency in economic relations. Sovereignties tend to be shaped by equality and cooperation, rather than by domination and conflict. Productive specialization does not contradict economic autonomy. Economic evolution focuses on the attainment of maximum feasible welfare. In the Argentine case, the trajectory resulting from such an objective implies important structural changes and realization of a high growth potential. Trade patterns change rapidly, with increasing concentration in dynamically efficient industries. The economy tends to become a net creditor in the medium-long run.

Later on, when the process of adjustment to global openness is confronted with frictions that limit the feasible growth of exports, income growth and welfare are reduced, and the resulting changes in output and trade patterns decrease in importance. Traditional exports of agricultural goods retain a significant position, along with new, dynamically efficient economic activities.

These are the main themes of this book. We hope that by having conveyed its general purpose and flavour, we have whetted the reader's appetite to become more acquainted with it in the following chapters.

PART I
FOUNDATIONS

2 Environment

Key descriptors of contemporary world economic conditions are *volatility, turbulence, uncertainty*. They express the effects of the ongoing rapid transformation of world economic structures on collective perception.

Uncertainty about future economic evolution reflects uncertainty about economies' modes of functioning and about the basic structure of relationships underlying economic phenomena. In turn, theoretic uncertainty about basic economic structures reflects the relative dilution of economic hegemony, that is, the current dispersion of economic dominance and its corresponding models of scientific or ideological explanation.

In this relatively chaotic environment, economic prediction beyond the very short run is a futile exercise. Turbulence is characterized by the absence of uniform, unique structures. Such a turbulent situation may be described as a region of potential bifurcations, an interval of resolution or revelation of new modes of evolution. Contours of latent configurations can only be deduced as different modes of resolution, i.e., ways of resolving accumulated tension.

In this chapter, through analysis of existing disequilibria in the contemporary world economic environment, we try to discern virtual configurations, or scenarios, resulting from different modes of resolution. In later chapters, we study optimal strategies for adaptation to each emerging type of international economic environment.

Technical revolution and comparative advantage

The most important and most dynamic component of the contemporary technological revolution is microelectronics, as applied to the storage, processing and transmission of information.[1] Microelectronic applications have accelerated the rate of change in nearly all production technologies. Different forms of microelectronics-based automation are progressing in every sphere of production. In conjunction with new communications technologies (satellites, optical fibres, etc.), microelectronics allows for massive exchange of information between points anywhere on the globe at the velocity of light. While accelerated technical change increases the importance of information and knowledge as productive factors, the new technologies increase the availability and potential accessibility of the existing stock of knowledge (bibliographic and data banks, etc.).

The evolving technical paradigm decreases the importance of the scale of production, and possibly even creates an effect of scale diseconomies in branches where new technologies are particularly viable. Automatized production processes are often modular, with small productive units which are profitably operable at low output volumes. Process configurations can change; there is flexibility.[2]

The 'third industrial revolution' also sways the technological foundations of agriculture, with the application of genetic manipulation techniques to develop varieties with desired properties (yields, resistance to drought, plague, etc.).[3]

But the area where the introduction of new technologies has produced the most dramatic, although perhaps less visible, effects on the world economy is in international financial markets. Today, telematics assure instant contact and permanent intercommunication among world financial markets. Five hundred billion electromagnetic dollars glide across national borders every day in the form of different financial transactions. Stock markets have also become increasingly integrated, and their signals are transmitted to each other

---

[1] The explosive development of this technology may be illustrated by the following example: in the early 1960s a computer executed 34 thousand mathematical operations in one second; 20 years later this figure was 800 million. The cost of the microprocessor diminished by 90 per cent in the same period. See e.g. Hagedoorn, Kalff and Korpel (1988).

[2] For a detailed description of the emerging 'systemofacture' labour process, see e.g. Kaplinsky (1989).

[3] Biotechnologies and their implications for agricultural development are discussed in e.g. Fowler et al. (1988).

instantaneously. Nowadays there is an integrated, largely supranational capital market.

Technical developments of the past decades will necessarily influence production costs and tendencies towards specialization among economies. The importance of information and knowledge as productive factors is increased by new technologies; knowledge-intensive industries are the most expansive in this period of intense technological change. Economies with a relative abundance of well-qualified technicians and scientists and, not less important, with appropriate technical infrastructure and social institutions, may be regarded as relatively advantaged in the production of knowledge-intensive goods and services.

The fact that, in contrast to the high technologies of the past (steel, chemicals, etc.), new technologies diminish the weight of the scale of production as a cost-reducing factor has implications for location trends and comparative advantage. The size of a particular market loses some of its relative importance as a determinant of location of production based on applications of new technologies. Firm size and scale of production are less important than technological absorption capacity.

The ongoing technical revolution seems to affect relative prices of agricultural and other commodities in the sense that they will continue to diminish. The long run trend of declining real prices of commodities (excluding oil), and the trend towards terms-of-trade deterioration in commodity exporting countries will persist. The new 'green revolution' resulting from applications of biotechnology will probably prolong the tendency towards decreasing weight of the 'land' factor – that is, of fertile soil and suitable climate – in determining comparative costs of agricultural output. This, of course, does not exclude the possibility that land-abundant economies currently specialized in agricultural production can maintain a (declining) relative advantage for some time.

Technological irruption and regulability

The impact of technological developments in financial markets has implications for basic aspects of the functioning of national economies. Global 'telematization' of stock, exchange and credit markets has become the vehicle of new types of financial operations, new credit instruments and new mechanisms for international transfer of assets, resulting in international integration of financial markets. This has implied the emergence of a global, supranational financial system, largely beyond the control of monetary authorities.[4]

In this new financial world, the familiar instruments and models of traditional macroeconomic policy have become nonoperational. Prior to financial deregulation, in the context of the financially closed economy, the function of monetary policy has been to maintain an interest rate level which assures a high degree of economic activity, consistent with acceptable inflation levels.[5] In this framework, the quantity of money and credit are instruments of monetary policy which can be regulated, within certain limits, in order to maintain, also within certain limits, desired interest rate levels. With financial deregulation and capital market globalization, the situation changes. In the open monetary economy, interest rates prevailing in each economy cannot conspicuously or durably diverge from one other, once they have been adjusted by the expected variation in respective exchange rates and by other perceived risks (controls, confiscation, etc.). Capital flows between economies tend to equalize financial returns so adjusted.

In these circumstances, the function of monetary policy is reduced to ensuring an acceptable or sustainable evolution of external indebtedness, that is, to assure an equilibrium in capital movements. Any attempt to force interest rates below or above their 'natural' level produces paradoxical or perverse effects. An increase in the rate of interest above its 'natural' level, for instance, gives rise to an inflow of capital, an increase in the monetary base and an expansion of the quantity of money and credit. But a higher interest rate also has recessive effects, through the contractive effect on investment. The expansive effect of increased liquidity along with the recessive effect of reduced investment generate the 'stagflation' syndrome.

The open macroeconomy of today has also eroded the basis of traditional Keynesian fiscal policy. International linkage of financial markets has reduced the possibilities of influencing levels of economic activity through

[4] In this light, the worldwide financial deregulation of the past decade can equally well be regarded as a spontaneous process of obsolescence and deactivation of a set of institutions, norms and rules of functioning whose object of application has totally changed, as the result of deliberate application of a particular doctrine of economic policy.

[5] Although less generally recognized, another function of monetary policy in the closed economy is to regulate the distribution of income, through its effect on the rate of profits. 'The rate of profits, as a ratio, has a significance which is independent of any prices, and can well be "given" before the prices are fixed. It is accordingly susceptible of being determined from outside the system of production, in particular by the level of the monetary rates of interest.' (Sraffa, 1960, p. 33.)

noncompensated public spending.[6] For instance, the perception that a fiscal deficit will not be financed by internal saving, or that it may have inflationary effects, will increase the interest differential and provoke net capital inflows, with the 'stagflationary' consequences described above. Changes in the international environment have thus tended to dilute the efficacy of the traditional instruments of macroeconomic policy. The regulative capability of national economic policy has been eroded. Magnitudes such as interest and exchange rates, crucial for the functioning of the national economy, are now determined in international financial markets, that is, by an supranational system, beyond the regulatory power of national states. The turbulence of the world economy since the mid-1970s may thus be seen as the effect of continuous shocks to institutional systems by a massive complex of technical innovations, or as the stresses and strains of rapid technological change which confront stagnating or decaying governing systems and institutions.[7]

The erosion of nation-states' regulatory capabilities and the constitution of a supranational economic and financial system actualize — at a higher, global level — old questions formerly posed at the level of the national economy. Is the global economic system efficient ? Is it stable? Is it equitable? Does it have inherent tendencies towards unemployment?

Increasing tensions in the world economy

The process of technological irruption briefly described above had a major role in the generation of tensions and disequilibria which — in a context of relative global stagnation — characterized the world economy since the mid-1970s. During the period in question, the accelerated technological absorption process is intimately related to the evolution of a central factor in the regulation of the global economic system, i.e., the rate of interest.

---

6 This refers to industrialized economies. The structural origin of unemployment and the relative irrelevance of this type of fiscal policy in less developed economies have long been acknowledged; see e.g. Kalecki (1960).

7 'There appears to be a fundamental lag between the current rate of technological change and the rate of adjustment to these changes among decision-makers. Technology that evolves much more rapidly than the body politic can absorb creates strain and stresses which lead to dislocations, instabilities and paralysis of action — and sometimes perverse responses.' (Blumenthal, 1988, pp. 531-2.) These words, which seem to paraphrase the Preface to the *Contribution to the Critique of Political Economy,* were written by an outstanding agent in this process, the chairman of a worldwide computer-producing corporation.

As we have seen, globalization of capital markets throughout this period resulted in autonomization of interest rates at the national economy level; interest rates are not amenable to control by national monetary authorities. The rate of interest becomes an endogenous variable at the level of the global economy, beyond the influence of national monetary authorities, including those of the largest economies.

The initial impulse to the present technological wave seems to have been given by tendencies towards declining profit rates (and increasing real wages) which, although continually present since the 1960s, were progressively accentuated until the late 1970s.[8] This was a period of low and declining real rates of interest. In the mid-1970s, real interest rates became negative, due to the dramatic increase in international liquidity from surpluses of the oil-exporting countries.[9]

Decreasing profit rates and increasing real wages augment the pressure in favour of labour-saving technologies, while declining real interest rates make the cost of introducing innovations embodied in new machinery and equipment relatively cheaper. This basic mechanism of the accumulation process explains the reversion, in the late 1970s, of the preceding tendencies, with recovery of profit rates, stagnation or decline of real wages and higher unemployment.[10] Since then, real interest rapidly increased to unprecedented levels, which have dominated the entire decade of the 1980s.[11]

This description is, obviously, a schematic portrayal of the global economic process as spontaneous, fundamentally governed by impulses from the economy which give rise to acceleration of technical change. Technical change, in turn, brings forth a process of reaccommodation within the economy and its interrelations with other economies.[12]

---

[8] In the seven largest economies of the OECD (Group of Seven), operating surplus as a percentage of gross value added in manufacturing has decreased from an (unweighted) average of 35.7 per cent in 1960-67 to 34.2 per cent in 1968-73 and 30.6 per cent in 1974-79; the average rate of increase in real wages in manufacturing was 3.5, 4.4 and 1.5 per cent, respectively (OECD, 1988, Tables 7.2 and 9.4).

[9] For the Group of Seven, average real long term interest rates declined from 2.1 per cent per annum in 1960-67 to 1.3 per cent in 1968-73 and -0.2 in 1974-79 (ibid., Table 10.10).

[10] The operating surplus in the Group of Seven increased in 1980-85 and the average was 31.5 per cent; the rate of change in real wages was 0.7 per cent (ibid., Tables 7.2 and 9.4).

[11] The average for the Group of Seven was 4.3 per cent in 1980-86 (ibid., Table 10.10). It remained at about that level during the rest of the 1980s (see e.g. OECD, 1991, various issues).

[12] For alternative approaches to 'long waves' along lines similar to these, see Di Matteo and Goodwin (1989) and Goodwin and Puzzo (1987).

In this epoch of financial deregulation and capital market globalization, the general increase in real interest rates – made possible mainly by the increase in rates of profits – cannot be regarded as the result of having applied some specific monetary policy. An overriding feature of the existing monetary system is precisely the absence of international regulating authorities.[13]

The US economy, however, due to its relative weight and the type of policies applied, has had a special role in the evolution of the global level of interest rates. The US economy has led the process of increasing interest rates starting in the mid-1970s, and maintains — at a high level — a positive differential against other economies. The origin of this differential can easily be traced to the fiscal policy applied: reduced public income (resulting from a distributionally regressive tax reform) combined with increased expenditure (basically military expenditure).[14]

The large budget deficit thus generated has to be financed through increasing debt, which represents a substantial addition to the demand for credit.[15] The US interest differential gives rise to large capital inflows and pressure to appreciate the dollar. The progressive 'overvaluation' of the dollar above the level of trade equilibrium leads to rapidly increasing imports, stagnating exports and a large trade deficit.[16] Real appreciation continued until 1985; at that point, the expected depreciation of the dollar exceeded the interest differential of dollar-denominated assets, and the dollar gradually declined to its predeficit level of the late 1970s.

Depreciation of the dollar, however, did not succeed in reversing the US trade deficit, and perhaps cannot achieve this by itself. Foreign trade equilibrium requires changes in underlying factors, such as the fiscal deficit and the insufficiency of internal saving. Given the low level of domestic saving, the fiscal deficit has ultimately been financed by external borrowing. After having been the largest international creditor in the early 1980s, the US

---

[13] Since the Second World War and until 1971 — a period characterized by fixed exchange rates — the International Monetary Fund had somewhat of a regulatory role which was radically eroded by the subsequent general floating of exchange rates.

[14] The rate of increase in real military expenditure in the US jumped from 0.7 per cent per annum in 1975-80 to 7.1 per cent in 1980-85. For the other NATO members combined, the rates were 2.4 and 1.8 per cent, respectively. (SIPRI, 1984 and 1986, Tables 3A.1 and 11A.2.)

[15] The US budget deficit reached almost 200 billion dollars in the mid-1980s, about 6 per cent of GNP.

[16] The trade deficit reached a magnitude comparable to that of the budget deficit in the mid-1980s.

economy has thus abruptly become the largest debtor in the late 1980s, with a debt comparable to that of the total debt of all third world countries.[17]

Thus, the US economy has led the present phase of recovery of real interest rates accompanying the global process of rising profit rates and decelerating or decreasing real wages. The general ascent of interest rates has the most serious impact on less developed economies, where interest rates reach very high levels – higher than expected return levels of most productive investment projects. In these circumstances, and when financial markets are interconnected, the tendency towards 'capital flight' increases. A non-negligible part of the US budget and trade deficit was thus financed by capital flows from developing countries.[18]

Some economists compare the situation created by this powerful financial gravitational field with the bewildering conditions surrounding the black holes of cosmic space.[19] Accumulated tensions and disequilibria in the world economy seem to reach saturation levels, and to indicate possible discontinuities and changes in evolutionary regime. In the vicinity of such potential bifurcation points, it is only possible to trace the conceivable contours of alternative reconfigurations of the world economic system.

Vistas of the world economy

Massive irruptions of technical innovations have shaken the world economy for more than a decade and have given rise to a global economic and financial system. The system lacks global regulatory rules and mechanisms. Operation of the system has eroded existing, nationally based regulation capabilities. The growing lag between (global) technologies and (local) institutions generates instability and heightens tensions. For the time being, the most notorious reflection of disequilibrium is the US external debt. This exposes

[17] In 1985, the net international investment position of the US showed a minus of 111 billion dollars (UN, 1989, Table IV.5). Calculated in the same way as debt statistics for developing countries, i.e., gross foreign claims excluding direct investment and foreign holdings of equity shares, the US debt amounted to 1.3 trillion dollars in 1988, that is, the same order of magnitude as the total debt of less developed economies (UN, 1989, p. 84).

[18] Of a total net transfer of resources to the US of 834 billion dollars in 1982-89, 292 billion, i.e., 35 per cent, came from developing countries. Latin America accounted for 38 per cent of the financial resources from the less developed countries. (UN, 1990, Table IV.7.)

[19] See Thurow and D'Andrea Tyson (1987).

the dollar, and the global financial and monetary system based on it, to a widening credibility gap and to increasing instability.

These alarming signals are sometimes interpreted as being full of disruptive power. According to one scenario, the world economy will be precipitated into a depression, with massive economic dislocation. The effects of this collapse, however, need not necessarily be negative in all cases.

Enlarged perception of the risks involved in international economic fragmentation might also initiate a process of reconstruction of international institutions, towards a more stable, open and equitable global system. This scenario might be the result of rational persuasion about the benefits of cooperation, or also the consequence of limited or minor verifications of the dislocation scenario.

Most mainstream expectations, as reflected by international economic organizations, are situated somewhere between these two scenarios. In such intermediate scenarios, tensions are prolonged and stagnation persists.

Fragmentation

The depreciation of the dollar since 1985 has not gone so far as to eliminate the US trade deficit.[20] Perhaps depreciation is not even effective enough as an instrument when the deficit has deep-rooted, structural causes. Fiscal deficits and concern about inflation induce restrictive monetary policy and high interest rates. The global investment level is low and perceived investment opportunities are limited. These elements conform to a recessive context. Given this general recessive background, the US trade deficit and accumulated debt are the focus of worried attention.

In this scenario, the panic originates in a sudden reversal of expectations about the dollar, that is, about the debt repayment capacity of the US economy.[21] When expectations are reversed, there is a run away from the dollar and other dollar assets, the so-called 'hard landing'.[22] The financial stampede out of the US economy provokes a rise in interest rates, which has

---

[20] The US trade deficit diminished in the second half of the 1980s at a declining rate, seemingly approaching zero. That is, the deficit seems to have stabilized around 120 billion dollars (OECD, 1991, various issues).

[21] More recently, expectation reversals and panics already seem to have occurred. They were compensated by large-scale dollar acquisitions by central banks. In 1987, central banks bought an estimated 85 billion dollars in support of the dollar (UN, 1989, p. 91).

[22] The classic statement of the hard landing scenario is due to Marris (1987). Batra (1985) proposed another depression scenario, deduced from long run time series.

to be large enough to induce a fall in investment, output and imports, in turn capable of rapidly producing a trade surplus equivalent *ex post* to the net capital outflow. The depth of the depression depends on how sensitive the trade balance is to the dollar exchange rate. The remaining adjustment then has to be generated by a fall in the activity level and in imports. The required rise in the interest rate will depend on the interest elasticity of investment demand. The rise in interest rates has to be large enough to generate a reduction in the volume of investment, income and imports required to finance the capital outflow.[23]

Dollar devaluation has a direct inflationary impact by increasing prices of imported goods. The indirect inflationary pressure of the fiscal deficit – until now contained through external indebtedness — shows up in full force. Inflation is functional in reducing real wages and consumption, and in generating the savings surplus which finances net capital outflows. From the 'hard landing' onwards, the budget deficit is increasingly financed through the inflation tax. Thus latent stagflation abruptly turns into open, Latin American style 'depreflation'. Inflation, however, has one mitigating effect. External debt, mostly denominated in dollars, liquefies in direct proportion to the inflation rate.[24]

In these circumstances of high unemployment and large financial disruption, economic policy activism regains acceptance. A new consensus is gained for active foreign trade policies, financial reregulation and Keynesian macropolicies.[25]

The malady rapidly spreads to all economies, central and peripheral, closely linked as they are by trade and finance. The first depressive impulses are transmitted through exchange and money markets, with similar cycles of increasing interest rates, falling investment, incomes, imports, etc. The trend away from economic openness is a spontaneous effect of declining incomes and demands for imports, and also a consequence of escalating protectionism. 'Strategic trade policy' and protectionism are elements of comprehensive

[23] Marris (1987, p. 137) estimated the required drop in GDP in the OECD countries to be 4 per cent.

[24] 'The temptation for America simply to inflate its way out of its debt problem, as many other large debtors have done in history, will be strong, perhaps irresistible.' (Thurow and D'Andrea Tyson, 1987, p. 20.)

[25] At different levels of development, such tendencies are already present. Increasing protectionism, and the emergence of bilateralism and managed trade in the 1980s are well documented (see e.g. UNCTAD annual reports). The current trend towards currency zones and monetary unification is an incipient symptom of reregulation. Keynesianism (in its 'neo', 'new' and 'post' varieties) is gaining ground, although still only at the theoretical level.

national economic strategies for expanding self-regulating capabilities. These strategies are structured around themes such as the internal market, investment, industry, employment and education-research-innovation.

Fragmentation of the global system does not go so far as to detach each national economy. The process may stop at the level of economic blocs or zones.[26]

In this scenario, the tension between global techno-productive systems and local regulatory structures leads to, and is resolved by, depression. As it fractures global techno-productive systems, depression also enlarges the governability of national economies. Within the resulting reduced economic spaces, the technological systems whose irruption initially provoked the convulsive reaction of the crisis are assimilated in a more orderly and regular way.[27]

The *dénouement* of crisis and dislocation brings forth some positive consequences for third world economies, particularly for highly indebted economies. Disruption of the international payments system along with reintroduction of capital and exchange controls reveal the international, political side of the debt problem. External debt positions and servicing depend closely on the evolving configuration of interest and power balances among states. In an environment characterized by changing collusion (and collision) patterns among states, managed trade and limited convertibility, debt volumes and debt servicing depend on negotiated deals which may take many different forms.[28]

Global financial disruption and reregulation of international capital flows block the drain of investable resources represented by trade surpluses.[29] The interruption of nonregistered outflows of financial resources ('capital flight') is

---

[26] It is natural to conceive of a fracture along existing lines: the US (and the rest of the Americas as a dollar zone), the European Community (including Africa as its zone of influence) and Japan (as the dominating nucleus of East Asia).

[27] In the scenario outlined by Michel Aglietta (1985, p. 54): 'The fracturing of the world economy is certainly the result of a great crisis. But it is also the crucible where new economic structures are melted, the cauldron where the ingredients of a new regime of growth are boiled, the ground of great technical revolutions.'

[28] This description brings to mind the environment of the 1930s; see e.g. Díaz Alejandro (1983). Some authors see more resemblance with the great depression of the last *fin de siècle,* which generated the colonial system and culminated in the First World War; cf. Boyer (1986, Chapter 8).

[29] Net capital flows to developing (capital importing) countries became negative in 1983. The accumulated net transfer of financial resources from developing countries to developed countries in 1983-89 was 204 billion dollars, of which 86 per cent is attributed to Latin America (UN, 1990, Table IV.1).

of similar importance. Increased inflows of direct investment also result from strategies emphasizing reindustrialization and market expansion.

This type of fragmentation scenario admits two main alternative forms of realization. In the first form, technological deployment exploits the potential capacity of new technologies for increasing individual control and initiative in the work process. Enlarged capabilities and autonomy, increased perception of the whole productive process, that is, relative disalienation within the labour process, coincide with relative disalienation of the process of appropriating economic surplus. Different micro and macroeconomic redistribution mechanisms are introduced so as to induce expanded technological absorption capacities.[30]

In this positive realization of economic introversion, economic growth translates into widely diffused welfare, with an even spread of technology among individuals, sectors and regions, and with multi-faceted expansion of productive and expressive capabilities.

In the alternative form of realization of the fragmentation scenario, industrialization and growth assume more compelling features. The nation-state is rediscovered among the debris of the technological tide, recomposed and elevated to the category of an entity or organism with its own interests and aims, over and above those of its members. The objectives which the state imposes on the economic system are national strength and autonomy. All other objectives potentially in conflict with those of the state – for instance, the distributive objective – are dismissed.

Technology, in this scenario, tends to be concentrated in the large firms which form the strategic kernel of the growth effort. Technology diffusion in the rest of the productive system is limited. This regime is not consistent with either stimulus to increased intelligibility and transparence of technical systems, or with creative intervention of labour in the work process. A correctly disciplined and subordinated labour force is more important.

Sociopolitically, this scheme is compatible with centralized, authoritarian, corporative organization, and perhaps incompatible with polycentric,

---

[30] In Aglietta's (1985, p. 55) words: 'If [the orientation given to technical progress] allows for enriching the content of negotiated agreements between employers and wage earners, if it extends the wage earner's responsibility at work, the transformation of productive systems will give a new impulse to social progress.' There has been, in recent years, a proliferation of studies and proposals of workers' participation schemes as a means of reversing stagflation, by increasing the motivation and productivity of labour and diminishing the inflationary pressure originating in the distributive struggle. See e.g. Foster (1987), Meidner (1978), Vines, Maciejowsky and Meade (1983) and Weitzman (1984).

democratic institutions. If the democratic system fails to discern the internal and external symptoms of the crisis and dislocation of the international system, and to articulate the responses required in order to conduct economic regulation effectively within free and progressive institutions, it is not impossible that new national-messianic constellations could impose their will on societies prostrated by paralysis or despair.

Integration

In the preceding scenarios, tensions arising from evolutionary lags between techno-productive and governing systems fracture the global system into governable (or even 'hypergovernable') fragments. Another potential, symmetric *dénouement* alternative is an evolutionary leap of the global system. It implies the gestation of a global system of rules and institutions, which increase global stability and adaptability. This seems to be the great task and evolutionary challenge of the present *fin de siècle*.[31]

This mutation is invoked from the techno-productive system itself. Within it are perceived the growing risks of instability and fragmentation, as well as the possibilities contained in free global expansion.[32] Although still not very effective, the initiatives emanated from different international organizations are more understandable and natural, since dislocation would question their own existence.[33]

As in the fragmentation scenario, two main types of realizations of the global regulation system can be discerned. In the first type, acknowledged loss of control at the national economy level leads to agreement on the necessity of global regulatory instruments and institutions. A reconstructed

---

[31] 'The central bifurcation dominating the end of the 20th century is that in the absence of a hegemony relation, a new form of international organization might evolve through negotiation.' (Mistral, 1986, p. 198.)

[32] 'We need to define a bold and comprehensive new philosophical underpining for the management of domestic and international economic affairs, a kind of new economic *Weltanschauung* that explicitly recognizes the new problems but also the enormous opportunities for mankind which technology has opened up. What I have in mind is a general framework for the gradual restructuring of domestic and international economic relations that corresponds more closely to the technological realities of our day.' (Blumenthal, 1988, p. 547.)

[33] In recent years, there has been increased interest in the problem of macroeconomic policy coordination; see e.g. the IMF study by Guth (1988). An intractable problem, which precludes definite theoretical results, is the so-called 'uncertainty about the underlying economic model', an effect, ultimately, of the relative dispersion of economic hegemony.

international system establishes effective powers of legislation, jurisdiction and administration, in part delegated by its members. The movement is similar to that which, in the past, led to the constitution of nation-states, as a response to underlying economic necessities of the time. The new global *polis* conforms to a single economic space, with a common currency and a common budget which finances the production of global public goods and promotes a just and efficient allocation of global resources.[34]

The most important global public good is security. The level of worldwide military expenditure is the clearest symptom of insecurity and irrationality in the international system.[35] In a world with police forces solely at the local level, global security can be assured by a small fraction of present military costs. Reductions in military expenditure could finance additions to development aid.[36]

Global integration and *détente* coincide with rapid reduction in military outlays, thereby neutralizing one of the main factors of international economic tension: the US budget deficit and the growing external indebtedness associated with it.[37]

Other fundamental goods provided by the global *polis* are a basic set of rules and norms of conduct, and their corresponding mechanisms for application and jurisdiction. They comprise basic civil and political rights, the environment and common resources, and international transactions. Stable realization of international competition and full liberalization of trade require global regulation mechanisms. The most basic of these is monetary

---

[34] The South Commission (1990) is a recent proposal in this direction. See also Tinbergen and Fischer (1987) and Streeten (1991). Several initiatives towards world government and United Nations' reform are reported in Ferencz and Keyes (1988).

[35] World military expenditures grew in the 1980s to an unprecedented level of an estimated one trillion dollars in 1987 (data from the US Arms Control and Disarmament Agency, quoted in World Bank, 1990, p. 17).

[36] A 10 per cent reduction in world military expenditures is equivalent to triplication of official development assistance (33 billion dollar receipts in 1989, according to World Bank, 1991, Table 20).

[37] 'All along, U.S. deficits have been in large measure a consequence of America's willingness to carry the heaviest share of the defense burdens of the noncommunist world. An end to the American deficits suggests an end to the American burdens. This gives the present financial crisis a geopolitical and historical dimension.' (Calleo et al., 1988, p. 846). For Lester Thurow, military effort is a basic explanation for structural problems in the American economy: 'Having essentially taken defense out of investment ever since World War II, the consequences have now caught up with us to produce an uncompetitive economy.' (Thurow, 1985, p. 123.)

regulation, which implies a common currency and a central monetary authority.[38]

Exchange-rate uncertainty, a main component of current economic uncertainty, is thus dissipated. A single currency and common, stable rules of conduct, ensure increased efficiency in the global allocation of investment, and a tendency towards international equalization of labour rewards. This is not sufficient, however, to eliminate huge existing disparities. Monetary unification and liberalization of trade are accompanied by mechanisms for the transfer of resources and technology to the less developed regions.[39] The resulting expansion of investment demands compensates the fall in military expenditure.[40]

An institutional mutation process provides the techno-productive system with an extended evolutionary environment. Increased coherence with the regulatory system guarantees its continued global development. In contrast with techno-military deployment, development in the multi-dimensional space of human capabilities is sustainable, and in principle unlimited. A large share of the energies and capacities now invested in military research may be converted into even more ambitious and technically advanced projects for global integration and human development.[41]

Such a mutation naturally affects structures, such as the military-industrial complex, that may be considered central elements of the former production and regulation regime, and are consequently part of the resistance mechanism. This mechanism is less operative if it can be smoothly incorporated – at least in its nonobsolete components – into the new evolutionary process.

The same occurs with some very specific segments of local governing systems (customs authorities, etc.). Within productive systems, relatively less

---

[38] Cf. the suggestion of a world central bank in Blumenthal (1988, p. 549). The idea of a common currency linked to a commodity buffer stock scheme — some sort of 'commodity standard' – is already found in Keynes (Kaldor, 1983). For some, less far-reaching, proposals from the 'Southern' Group of 24, see Dell (1987).

[39] Classic proposals in the direction of global welfare policies include Brandt et al. (1980, 1983). Herrera et al. (1976) is a seminal Latin American contribution to global welfare modeling. More recent formalized analyses are e.g. Costa (1983) and Granberg and Rubinshtein (1984).

[40] Leontief and Duchin (1983) analyzed the disarmament-development link within an input-output model of the world economy. See also Royer (1986).

[41] 'New initiatives [for reconstructing the global institutional framework] can become more acceptable within such a framework if seen as part of a general new strategy to bring the benefits of technology to all in an interdependent world.' (Blumenthal, 1988, p. 548.) 'We should not shy away from thinking about entirely new techniques and ideas, even if they may at first seem as revolutionary as the development of the microchip itself.' (Ibid., p. 549.)

dynamic activities and sectors, which may or may not coincide with highly protected sectors, also tend to be in opposition.[42] However, capitalists and workers with class — rather than branch or trade — consciousness tend to see the long-run benefits of general economic expansion and international equalization of living standards. Generalization of information, knowledge and modern means of production appeal to the professional middle class. Small informal trades and services may also benefit from technical advances and open economies' increased reliance on services.

Gestation of worldwide regulation systems is an evolutionary response to pressures inherent in technological globalization. This is a historical process with irregularities, accelerations and reversals. It does not exclude, for instance, the possibility of limited realization of the fragmentation scenario.

Another plausible irregularity of the globalization process, which represents a variant of the integration scenario, is constitution of an ad hoc global *polis* by the techno-productive system itself. Social disarticulation and political anomy resulting from technological shocks preclude attainment of the critical mass required to initiate the process of globalization of sociopolitical mechanisms. The amount of centrifugal force needed to initiate the fragmentation process cannot be attained either. In this uncertain environment, the techno-productive system develops rules and institutions required for a minimum of order.[43] The principle of regulation is maximal expansion of the global techno-productive system. Investments and financial resources flow according to that aim. Rates of profits and interest tend to equalize internationally, and real wages tend to converge internationally towards subsistence levels. There is no distributional concern at the global level, and it becomes highly restricted at the national level.

The system conforms to a global oligopoly, regulated by a global oligarchy.[44] It is an unstable, transitional form towards one of two alternative bifurcations. In the first case, coordination problems associated with obtaining

---

[42] A protected sector is not necessarily a dynamically inefficient sector; protection may be unnecessary (the industry generates high enough profits in the long run), or it may be transient (as applied to an infant industry).

[43] The Trilateral Commission, for instance, is apparently a nucleus with some regulatory role. There are also influential proposals for formalized mechanisms of restricted governance: 'It is important that there be both a forum where a limited number of large countries can make sensitive "bargains" and a forum in which the rest of the world can effectively communicate its views and concerns to the large countries.' (Crockett, 1988, p. 22.) Contemporary arrangements for international policy coordination seem to be evolving in this direction.

[44] Nikaido (1975) contains a theoretical analysis of collusive solutions within an oligopolistic system, e.g. through cooperative surplus-value maximization.

a cooperative solution of global oligopolistic competition give rise to coalitions around leading economies or blocs, that is, the transnational aspect of the global system eventually dominates its supranational aspect. This represents a return to some of the previous fragmentation scenarios.

In the other case, global oligopolistic collusion prevails; there is a cooperative search for a profit-maximizing equilibrium, with its tendencies towards wage equalization at subsistence levels. This in turn generates the social grounds and political pressure for democratizing global governing systems, and for 'upward equalization' of wages. This is thus a transitional form towards the more progressive variety of global *polis*.

Intermediate scenarios

In the face of the high uncertainty and fragility brought about by imbalances in the world economy, the basic tone of most prospective scenarios of the world economy is caution.[45] Increased uncertainty is reflected in less categorical, more overtly conditional economic forecasts.

The basic outlook for the world economy is prolongation of the trends of the 1980s. This is most clear in the case of industrial economies, for which an unchanged rate of growth is assumed in the 1990s.[46] A crucial assumption underlying this scenario is a decrease in real interest rates below their 1980s levels. Lower interest rates decrease the debt service burden and allow for slightly increased growth in developing countries, although below the earlier postwar trend. The basic outlook would not apply if the saving deficit of the US economy cannot be eliminated. Such demand pressure on global savings would maintain real interest rates at high levels, prolong current account imbalances and cause a threat to international financial stability.

Another main assumption of the basic outlook is the expected growth of exports from developing countries, at about the same rate as during the 1980s.

---

[45] The following description by the United Nations (1987, p. 4) is quite symptomatic: 'The present situation is highly precarious. It is universally recognized as unsustainable and the signs of strain are multiplying. It will be resolved one way or another, but an orderly resolution is preferable to one dictated by crisis in the market place or unilateral rejection of obligations.'

[46] See World Bank (1990, pp. 15-22). The *World Economic Outlook* (IMF, 1991) makes a similar forecast; in 1991-96 real output growth in the industrial economies will be close to the average rate of growth in the 1980s, i.e., substantially lower than in the earlier postwar period.

Failure to strengthen multilateral trade liberalization mechanisms, or extension of nontariff trade barriers, imply a second type of risk.

It could be said in conclusion that the basic expectations of international economic organizations are quite gloomy, and that they are conscious of the risks inherent in future global economic evolution. There seems to be low awareness of ways and opportunities for progress. Their current assessment of the adaptive potential of the global regulation system to which they belong appears to be rather pessimistic.[47]

[47] This sentiment is shared by outside observers: 'In the last analysis the problem is not so much the international system's organizational structures, but mainly the decision-makers' mental structures. These evolve much more slowly, and unfortunately learn only from shocks. International cooperation is a learning process, and as such it is in acute need of creativity and innovation.' (Elmandjra, 1988, p. 50.)

3 Method

Let us now turn to our study of strategic alternatives in the Argentine economy. Our basic tool is a model of the Argentine economy. This tool is an analytical structure and may be perceived as a logical fabric of relations among objects (variables) representing the essential characteristics of the way the economic system functions. The relationships among variables in the economic system are specified numerically, so as to represent the contemporary Argentine economy.

Our analytical focus is on the trends and potential for growth and structural change in the economy. We are concerned with the problem of how different modes and regimes for creating additional productive capacities and capabilities affect collective welfare, output structure and the pattern of trade specialization in the economy. A characteristic of this process is that the time scale over which it evolves is broad; in the process of economic development and structural change, relevant events ripen relatively slowly. Once they occur, they become less reversible. The necessary perspective is the medium or long run. We thus abstract from the temporary disequilibria of conjunctural evolution, and in particular from monetary disequilibria.

Even though the scale is enlarged, time intervenes in our study in a definite way. The model is dynamic, in the sense that it describes processes which happen in time; relevant events and their effects are situated in time in a coherent manner. One of the most important classes of events in our study consists of economic policy decisions. Time intervenes as a discrepancy or tension between policy objectives and actual circumstances. Different objectives give rise to different strategies and different time sequences of policy instruments, resulting in different evolutionary patterns for the economy. An optimal strategy is a strategy that obtains the highest level of fulfilment of the objective.

Our focus on structural change concerns two fundamental structures of the economic system: the output structure and the distributional structure. Analysis of specialization in international trade — or of import and export substitution in the case of the inwardly orientated economy — requires a relatively disaggregated approach. Assessment of the welfare effects of growth and structural change presupposes a distinction among different income groups.

The rest of this chapter is devoted to a diagrammatic description of the structure of the model used to generate the evolutionary scenarios in later chapters. The equations, variables and coefficients of the model are listed in Appendix 1. Estimation of the model coefficients with Argentine data is documented in Appendix 2.

Principle of motion

The basic principle of growth in the model is investment or capital accumulation, widely understood as the creation of productive capacities, physical and human, material and immaterial. This principle, sometimes called the acceleration principle, establishes a relationship between investment and output growth (or between output and existing capacities). Interpreting this relationship 'from the supply side', it may be said that the increase in production capacity (in one period) gives rise to an increase in output (in a later period). The effect of capacity increase on output growth depends on the magnitude of the increase in capacity on the one hand, and on its efficiency or output effectiveness on the other. This relationship between the rate of output growth, the efficiency of investment and the saving/investment propensity of the economy is known as the Harrod-Domar growth equation.[1]

---

[1] For a recent, thorough reformulation and validation of this type of theory, see Scott (1989).

The analysis assumes that the *ex post* identity between savings and investment also applies as *ex ante* equality. The focus is on the long run trend, and not on short run disequilibria which give rise to cycles of expansion and recession around the trend. This implies further that the volume of investment is not dependent on the unfathomable 'animal spirits' of entrepreneurs or capital owners, nor is it directly controllable by the government through fiscal policy. Autonomous variations in the level of investment can temporarily affect the activity level, but do not modify the long run growth potential of the economy. Given the long run focus of the analysis, we are concerned with the saving or surplus capacity of the economy; the sustainable saving level is the sustainable investment level.

The basic principle of motion for the economy is illustrated in Figure 3.1. Savings/investment in the period, which depend on output and income levels in that period, determine an increase in output. Gross outputs represented in the figure are to be understood as (a vector of) outputs of each of the sectors distinguished within the economy.

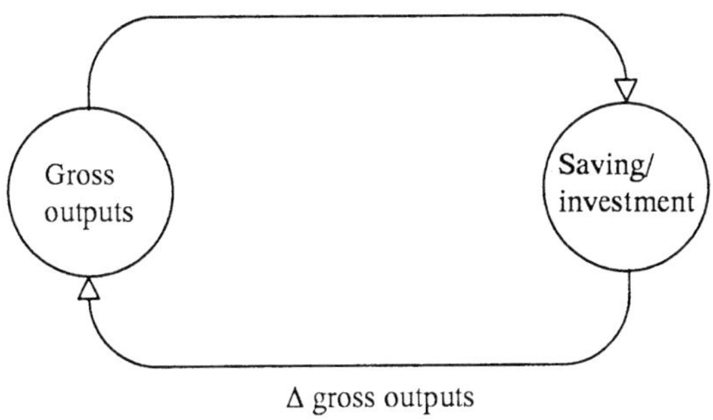

Figure 3.1

Instruments

After having shown the general principle of motion in the model, we can enhance the detail of the picture of the economic growth process by including the mechanisms that determine savings and investment, and the policy instruments which influence the structural evolution of the economy.

Figure 3.2 shows the functions that determine savings from outputs in one period, and the next period's outputs derived from sectoral investments. (That is, we assume that initial outputs are known.)

The upper part of the figure represents incomes generated in production. The upper box represents the function linking outputs to incomes. Income (value added) generated in each producing sector is distributed, according to known proportions, among income classes (where the government constitutes an income class).[2] This transformation thus determines disposable incomes of the different income classes and the income of the public sector (that is, direct and indirect tax revenues net of wage payments by the government, which add to private incomes).

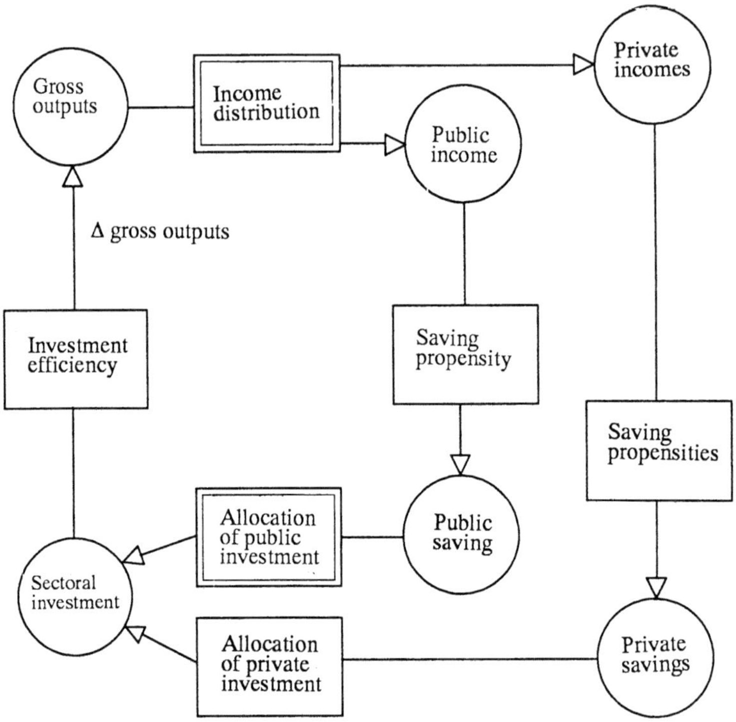

Figure 3.2

The double lines in the box representing the income distribution matrix mean that it is influenced by policy instruments. Economic policy influences

[2] Usually, the social accounting matrix (SAM) first depicts the distribution of value added among 'primary factors' (labour, capital, land), and then the distribution of factorial income among 'institutions' (households, firms, government). Household incomes are disaggregated into socioeconomic (or income) groups; see e.g. Pyatt and Round (1985). Due to the scarcity of income distribution data in Argentina, we do not consider factorial distribution, and sectoral value added is 'paid' directly to households and the government; see Clark (1975).

the structure of income distribution in various ways. Tax policy has a recognized distributional impact. Public expenditure also has redistributive effects, as benefits accruing from public expenditure differ among income classes. The redistributive effects of economic policy result from changes in the pattern of income flows, and from changes in the distribution of assets and productive capabilities (or their relative values).[3] These changes are reflected by changes in the shares of value added in each sector accruing to the different income classes. Within the framework of our model, a *distribution policy* is a time sequence of such income distribution coefficients, specified within a horizon of analysis.

The volume of savings generated in the economy depends on the level and distribution of income. Each income class has a particular accumulative behaviour; there are given, class-specific marginal propensities to save. When saving propensities differ among income classes, the level of domestic saving depends on the level of incomes, and on their distribution among income classes. Different distribution policies are thus associated with different volumes of saving, and consequently with different growth potentials.

According to our long run outlook, saving equals investment. This also applies for each institutional sector. In order to create productive capacities in the different sectors of activity, the public sector spends a volume of saving equal to the difference between public income (net of wages) and public consumption.[4] Private domestic saving equals private incomes less private consumption expenditures.

The next transformation, shown in the lower part of Figure 3.2, is the sectoral allocation of investment, private and public. The notion of public investment in our study applies to physical investments in infrastructure and in public and mixed enterprises, and to different forms of subsidization of

---

[3] A classic analysis of redistributive policies is Chenery (1974). Pyatt and Thorbecke (1976) and Thorbecke (1985) discuss methods for analyzing distributional effects within the SAM.

[4] We assume here a balanced public budget. The state may invest more than it saves by resorting to deficit financing. 'Crowding in' private investment through fiscal surplus is also suggested as a means of increasing investment in the present period of financial tightness; cf. Blejer and Cheasty (1986). Another way is to increase public saving and investment with a balanced budget. The cautious conclusion of Leff and Sato (1987, p. 574) is: 'Economists do not yet have many empirically based, practicable recommendations to offer decision-makers who might seek to institute a new regime of higher domestic saving rates in a Latin American country.' Their conclusions seem to share the approach of our study: '[F]uture studies may be more fruitful if they take a disaggregated approach to savings behaviour, and if they concentrate more on individual country studies than on cross-sectional analysis.' (Ibid., p. 575.)

investment activity.[5] The notion also applies to public expenditures usually understood as consumption expenditures (education, health), to the extent that they expand human productive capabilities.

Economic policy thus directly and indirectly influences the expansion of productive capacities, thereby modifying the structure of the economy. The weight or priority given to each particular sector is reflected in the share of public investment allocated to it. An *investment policy*, in our model, is a sequence of distribution coefficients of public investment funds allocated in every period to each of the producing sectors, within a given period of analysis. The double lines in the box in the lower part of Figure 3.2 mean that the allocation of public investment is an instrument of structural economic policy.

Private investments are allocated according to an endogenous mechanism. Private investments tend to concentrate in fast growing sectors, and in sectors with high 'capital requirements' (capital output ratios). Given the capital output ratio, the faster the growth in a particular sector, the larger the share of private investment allocated to it. This is the 'acceleration principle', now causally interpreted 'from the demand side'. This implies that private capitalists follow an adaptive strategy which indirectly responds to signals given by the public sector, through the effect of investment policy on output growth.[6]

The last transformation in the dynamic core of the model is the link between investment and output growth. Capacities added in each sector give rise to an output increase in the sector. There is a given relationship, particular to the sector, between additional production capacity and output growth. This is the incremental capital output ratio, which reflects the efficiency of investment.[7]

---

[5] 'Public funds devoted to investment have in the past been considerably larger than indicated by national income accounts. This has been the result of incentive regimes which dedicated a large part of public resources to subsidizing investments in the private sector, via tax exemptions and postponements.' (Argentina, 1985a, p. 57, note.)

[6] According to Tockman (1985), relatively passive behaviour is characteristic of Latin American entrepreneurs.

[7] The efficiency of investment is the inverse of the marginal capital output ratio, or marginal output capital ratio.

State variables

After having shown the factors that determine the rate and composition of output growth, we now focus on the relationships between economic welfare and output growth, and on the effects of growth on the pattern of foreign trade. These are included in the enlarged chart of Figure 3.3.

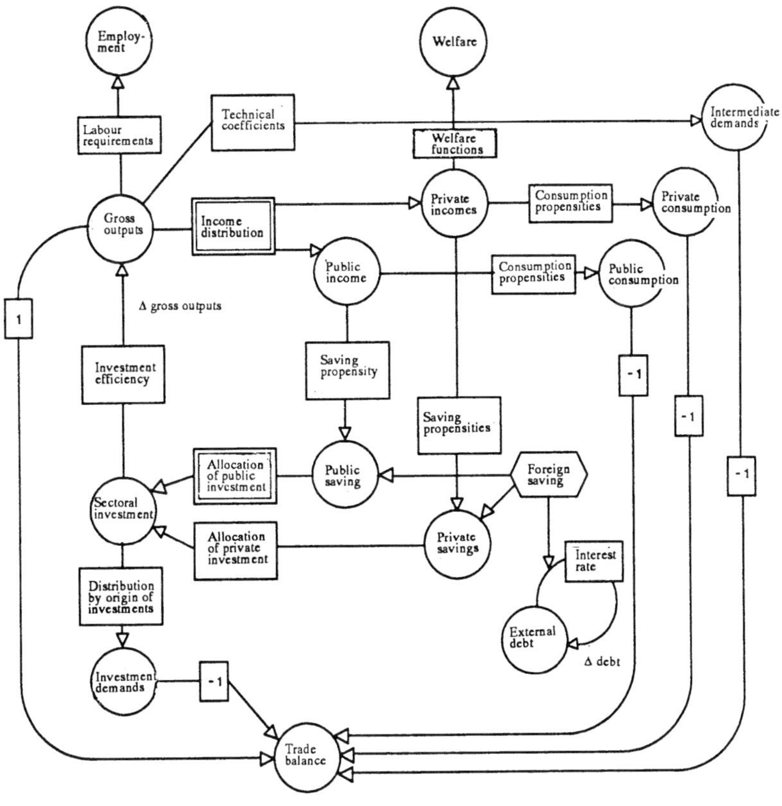

Figure 3.3

The notion of welfare enables us to rank the possible states of the economy according to their 'preferability'. One of the most frequently used interpretations of 'welfare' is the concept of real national income. This is the most common way of measuring and comparing the economic progress of nations. It is also a notion which has been widely criticized for including 'regrettables' such as defence expenditures, or neglecting the costs of environmental damage. Another serious objection against national income as a measure of welfare is that it is not sensitive to differences in the distribution of income. The same level of national income is compatible with equal income distribution, with total concentration, and so on. The rate of growth in national income is the weighted sum of the rates of income growth for the different individuals (or groups), where the weights are their respective shares in national income. For instance, when income is concentrated in one group, the growth rate of national income mainly reflects the income growth of that group.

One way of introducing a more equitable distributive judgement into the notion of national income is to assign the same weight in the social welfare function to the income growth of all individuals (or groups). This is the so-called 'democratic criterion' or 'equal weights' index.[8]

The reduction of poverty is another common way of assessing economic development. This can be incorporated into the welfare function by conferring a higher weight to lower income groups.[9] Another way of including a distributive concern in the welfare function involves correcting national income by an equality measure; we will call this measure the 'efficiency-equity' index.[10]

These four types of welfare functions, which depend on the level and distribution of incomes, are generically represented in the upper middle part of Figure 3.3.

The level and structure of employment associated with any output pattern is an important state variable, given widespread unemployment and under-employment. Different output configurations are associated with different employment configurations, given labour requirements by output unit in each sector of activity . These requirements are not constant, but change according to sectoral rates of labour productivity growth. Thus, the level and structure of employment may provide some additional qualitative insight by showing, for instance, the character (dualistic, homogeneous, etc.) of the process of development and structural change.

The next state variable, represented in the lower part of Figure 3.3, is the vector of sectoral trade balances, indicating the net imports or exports of each sector. Its temporal pattern reflects, for example, trends in 'import substitution', 'export substitution' and trade specialization. In our model,

---

[8] Pyatt and Thorbecke (1976). 'Welfare' in this case is a multiplicative – instead of an additive – function of individual incomes.

[9] Chenery et al. (1974, Chap. II).

[10] GDP times (one minus) the Gini coefficient; see Sen (1979).

sectoral excess demands are traded, that is, supplies in excess of domestic demand are exported, and excess demands over domestic production are supplied by imports. Different configurations of internal supplies and demands thus result in different patterns of sectoral foreign trade. The model describes a small open economy, in which the price system is exogenously given, i.e., world prices apply. Excess demands or supplies are channelled through external trade, instead of pressing prices up or down. This interpretation does not apply to sectors which produce nontradables. In those sectors, excess demands have to be interpreted as rationing situations.[11] Excess supplies are construed as idle or dissipated resources.

Sectoral trade balances are thus the difference, for each producing sector, between internal supplies (outputs) and demands. Given initial, historical sectoral outputs, the resulting evolution of outputs is derived from the dynamic law of the model for given policies, as described in the preceding section. Internal demands comprise three elements: intermediate, consumption and investment demands. Intermediate demands consist of goods and services used as inputs in production. Intermediate demands are linked to gross outputs through technical coefficients, that is, through given proportionality ratios between inputs and outputs (see the upper part of Figure 3.3). The second component of internal demand is consumption, in turn decomposed into private and public consumption demands. Consumption demands for each output category depend on disposable incomes for each income group (and the government). Sectoral consumption demands and disposable incomes are linked by marginal consumption propensities, specific to each income group (and the government).[12]

The third component of internal demand is investment demand. According to certain proportions specific to each sector, investments made in a sector are composed of investment goods originating in different sectors (machinery, construction, etc.). In other words, there are given proportionality relationships between sectoral investments (by sector of destination) and investment demands (by sector of origin).[13]

---

[11] When prices are rigid downwards and money supply is passive, rationing gives rise to 'structural inflation.' As concerns structural inflation theory and its Latin American roots, see Canavese (1982).

[12] This is the so-called extended linear expenditure system; see Lluch (1973). The system determines consumption and savings coefficients simultaneously, while the original linear expenditure system (Stone, 1954) determines the consumption basket only.

[13] See, for instance, Taylor (1975).

The sectoral balance of trade thus results from subtracting sectoral consumption (intermediate and final) and investment demands from sectoral gross outputs, as illustrated in Figure 3.3.

Sectoral trade deficits or surpluses add to the overall balance of trade in the economy. The overall trade deficit or surplus is, by construction, equal to the deficit or surplus savings of the economy (external saving or dissaving).[14] A trade deficit is an increase in the external liabilities of the economy, that is, an inflow of external resources (savings). A trade surplus represents a corresponding outflow of resources (external dissaving).

The overall trade or saving position of the economy is exogenously determined in our study as a given proportion of national income. It depends on the assumptions underlying each particular type of strategy or scenario, such as whether or not a fragmented or integrated payments system prevails. A hexagon in the lower right part of Figure 3.3 represents the exogenously determined amount of foreign saving.

Foreign saving (or dissaving) adds to (or is deducted from) the stream of internal savings, private and public. The private and public sectors absorb external savings (or repay their debts) in direct proportion to their respective share of internal savings.[15] At the same time, foreign savings (or dissavings) in each period add to (or deduct from) the external debt, whose initial value is known. In each period, interest is due on the external debt at a known rate.

Figure 3.4 is an overview of the whole model, now including the functions which allow for separate determination of imports and exports in each sector, shown in the lower part of the figure. In order to clarify the context of the equations, variables and coefficients listed in Appendix 1, we also introduce the mathematical notations in the figure.

---

[14] A proof of consistency is presented in Buzaglo (1984, Ch. 4). Strictly, both coincide only when all sectors produce tradables.

[15] This is an ad hoc hypothesis, due to the lack of information about exact behaviour.

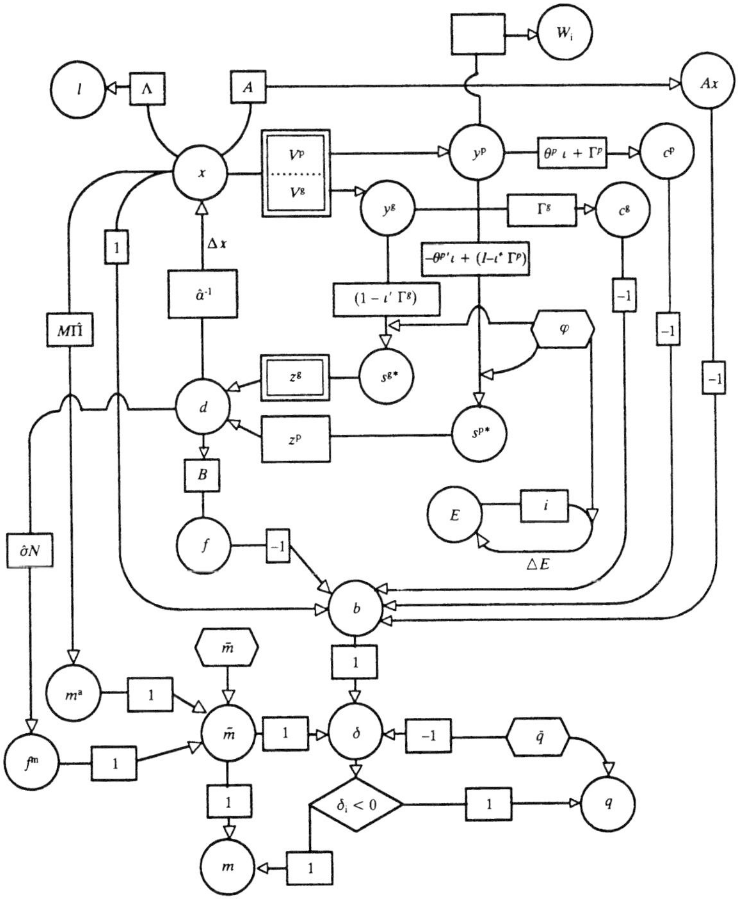

Figure 3.4

Sectoral trade balances may be understood as dependent on the supply/demand situation in each sector, for a given vector of prices, e.g. world prices. Exports and imports determined in this way may be termed 'competitive' exports and imports.

There are other factors which determine sectoral foreign trade. A certain proportion of inputs used in production is imported according to known coefficients. This demand for imported inputs m^a constitutes a first type of demand for 'noncompetitive imports'. A second type of noncompetitive imports is f^m, the demand for imported investment goods. This depends on sectoral investments, given coefficients of imported content in sectoral investments, and given coefficients of composition according to sector of origin of the investment goods imported by the sectors of destination. A third, exogenous component of demand for imports reflects the imports of consumption goods by sectors that are typically exporters.[16] These three components of 'noncompetitive imports', added to sectoral imports (the negative components of the trade balance vector), constitute m, total sectoral imports.

Total sectoral exports q are composed of sectoral net exports (the positive components of the trade balance vector) and of exogenous sectoral exports $\bar{q}$. Exogenous exports reflect exports by sectors which are typically net importers.[17]

Strategies

In the context of our study, a development strategy is a specific combination of an investment policy with an income distribution policy, for a given or planned evolution of foreign indebtedness. A strategy is a given time sequence of investment and distribution policy vectors, and of foreign saving coefficients, within a given horizon of analysis. Given this three sequences of coefficients and the initial gross outputs and foreign debt, the (numerically specified) model is recursively solved (integrated) along the period of analysis. This is usually called a simulation, or numerical experiment.

The simplest way of generating a strategy is to stipulate it exogenously. In the historical simulation, for instance, the model is solved starting at some initial period in the past and actual values of the policy variables are chosen. This type of experiment serves to assess the model's explicative power; if the solution accurately replicates past evolution, it can be said to have been validated by the facts, or at least not refuted by them.

Another way of generating strategies is optimization. Of all conceivable policy sequences, we select the one that accomplishes the maximal

---

[16] Agriculture, for instance, is a net exporting sector in Argentina; coffee and other tropical products not produced in Argentina are 'exogenous imports.'

[17] An example is exports of agricultural machinery by the typically net importing machinery sector.

achievement of an objective function. State variables are natural components of the objective function. For instance, for a given income distribution policy over time, we may wish to determine the investment policy sequence which maximizes welfare within the period. The resulting time pattern of the trade balances indicates the specialization effects of dynamically efficient structural change, or potential 'comparative dynamic advantages'.

The effects of a scenario of international economic fragmentation, or of a deliberate strategy of 'living off our means', can be explored by minimizing the vector of trade balances. For given distribution policies and zero debt repayments, for example, the problem would be to determine the investment policy sequence that sets sectoral trade balances as close to zero as possible.

In Part Two, the model is used as described here, first by historically simulating the period 1980-85, and then exploring different scenarios and strategies.

5 Stagnation

We turn now our sights to the future. In this and the following two chapters, the model is projected forward in time. Different ways of considering economic space-time reveal different evolutionary landscapes and itineraries. Stories developing in economic space-time depend on the structure of the model and on the ends of the main agents. Possible futures are innumerable: the future is not already given or contained in the past.

We propose several ways of illuminating the future, which imply different focuses of policy. Such focuses of policy may result from different strategic evaluations by an anthropomorphic rational state. They may also reflect the interests of different class or group coalitions. Or, they may result from *laissez-faire* adaptation to exogenous global conditions. These possibilities are not mutually exclusive.

Regardless of how they are determined, different ways of conceiving policy objectives result in different strategies of action, which in turn determine different future economic configurations, that is, different trajectories.

In this chapter, two aspects which characterize the decaying trend of the Argentine economy are assumed to be conserved: a high level of income concentration, and low levels of investment efficiency. The situation reflects uncertainties and tension in the global economic environment, compounded by conditions of internal structural fragility. It represents an intermediate situation of irresolution, with high real interest rates, net capital outflows from developing countries and protectionist policies in developed countries. The internal features are stagflation, divestment and ineffectiveness of economic policy.

One of the consequences of the assumptions is unsurprising: if the level of investment efficiency verified in the recent past is carried over into the future, the economy will continue to stagnate. Less unsurprising are the consequences of assuming, in this environment, a moratorium on external debt, or of attempting, in these circumstances, to 'live off our means', thereby drastically reducing the degree of economic openness.

Status quo and moratorium

The protracted economic crisis gives rise to increasing impatience about the heavy burden of external debt service, which is often seen as the sole or major cause of the crisis. It is then not surprising that programs for national economic salvation appear, with 'unilateral moratorium' as their sole or main content. It seems easier to unite behind the idea of correcting or eliminating effects attributed to an external cause, than to obtain a consensus to correct the effects of internal causes.[1]

In our first prospective experiment, we attempt to simulate the effects of such a moratorium, 'unilateral' in the sense that the only economic policy action endeavoured is the suspension of payments in terms of capital or interest on the external debt. This experiment is a projection of basic trends in the economy, with the exception of net capital outflows. That is, both investment and distribution policy prolong the tendencies of the recent past, while there is a reversal in foreign debt policy: payments are reduced to nil.[2] Consequently, potential accumulation capacity is augmented considerably.

Status quo and moratorium do not strictly constitute a strategy, as the policy adopted is not the result of a search for the maximum fulfilment of certain development ends, but is arbitrarily imposed. Moratorium can in principle be an element of many types of strategies.

Another aspect of this projection, which reflects status quo behaviour, refers to the efficiency of investments. Investment efficiency is assumed to be

---

[1] It seems as if the less democratic the prevailing political system is in practice, the greater the effectiveness of the resistance to this kind of 'social self-discipline'.

[2] The overall trade surplus (foreign dissaving) is then zero. This implies that capital flight is also zero, as we assume that the model accurately describes economic evolution.

the same as that which prevailed in the 1980s.[3] The environment in which investment activity evolves is about the same, and the internal and external factors which manifest themselves in low investment efficiency continue to operate.

The question then is: what would happen if, in the unchanged context of economic policies and behaviour, a debt moratorium were implemented?

To answer this question, an experiment is constructed, in which the model is solved for the next ten years, under the assumption that investment and distribution policies continue on the same course as in the past. The pattern of public investment policy throughout the ten-year period is similar to that of the first half of the 1980s, and the structure of income distribution remains unchanged.[4] The suspension of foreign debt payments implies the reduction of net capital outflows to zero, that is, balanced foreign trade.

According to the results of this experiment, the prospects of a 'unilateral moratorium' do not seem very promising. The substantial increase in internal saving and investment does not succeed in inducing output growth. All along the projection period, total output growth is about zero.[5] The increase in internal investment, however large, does not succeed in reverting the tendencies towards stagnation caused by low investment efficiency.[6] When the level of investment efficiency approaches zero, the volume of investment required to produce one additional unit of output tends to increase indefinitely. And as we have seen in Chapter 4 (Table 4.4), the levels resulting from simulation and adopted in this experiment are, with one exception, mostly zero (and negative in one case). For these efficiency levels, even a massive inflow of foreign capital as that experienced in the late 1970s would fail to reverse the tendencies towards stagnation in the economy.

At the sectoral level as well, the *Status quo and moratorium* alternative results in zero growth in most cases. An exception is machinery production, where a high negative investment efficiency coefficient prolongs the

---

[3] Investment efficiency coefficients used in this simulation are those that, along with foreign savings coefficients, best replicate actual development in 1980-85; see Chapter 4, Table 4.4.

[4] Coefficients of sectoral allocation of public investment in 1980-85 and historical income distribution coefficients are shown in Appendix 2.

[5] See Appendix 3, Table V.1. Numerical experiments in this study were carried out between 1986 and 1988, taking 1985 as the initial year (historical data) and 1985-95 as the simulation period. As long as stagnation persists, however, all experiments can be understood as simulating the effects of policies initiated in the current year (year 0).

[6] Let us recall that the average rate of foreign dissaving in 1980-85 was 3.3 per cent of GDP according to national account statistics, and 6.6 per cent according to Simulation IV (Chapter 4, Table 4.3).

declining trends in that sector. Another exception is energy production, where a positive (but less than unity) investment efficiency coefficient, along with high priority in public investment policy, result in the highest sectoral growth rate.

Status quo and moratorium results in practically unchanged output and demand patterns. External trade, which is a consequence of these factors, maintains a more or less unchanged pattern.[7] Relative specialization in agricultural exports is preserved. Industrial sectors continue to be net importers. The ratio between external trade and production is constant.

The results of this scenario may be summarized by stating that a moratorium on external debt, as an isolated policy measure, does not modify economic performance and/or the real external relations of the economy.

'Living off our means'

This experiment represents the first strategy simulation, in the sense defined in Chapter 3, as a sequence of economic policy actions aimed at reaching maximal realization of certain development objectives within a given policy horizon. The focus which now orients the configuration of the future economic landscape is the aspiration to achieve self-sufficiency in production. Of all conceivable evolutionary paths, we follow that which allows for maximum satisfaction of internal demands by internal production. The strategic objective or — in another interpretation — the evolutionary path imposed by external conditions, is to 'close' the economy or to 'live off our means' by substituting, to the greatest possible extent, domestic production for imports, and domestic consumption for exports. The suspension of foreign debt payments which this strategy involves is therefore less 'unilateral' than that assumed in the preceding *Status quo and moratorium* scenario.[8]

Two aspects of status quo prevail, however. First, distribution policy works in the sense of maintaining the existing distribution, which is thus regarded as the sole or best possible alternative. This, of course, is not inconsistent with the idea of adopting self-sufficiency in production as the strategic focus. Second, investment efficiency remains at the very low levels of the 1980s. As

---

[7] See Appendix 3, Table V.2.

[8] As in the preceding scenario, this simulation assumes balanced external trade, i.e., zero foreign dissavings, during the period.

in the preceding case, this reflects the persistence of the uncertain, stagnant environment of investment activity in that period.

Our question in this experiment is: what would be the consequences for the economy of adjustment to minimal openness, when external debt payments are interrupted, given unchanged efficiency in investment activity? Or, more specifically: within a horizon of 10 years, which investment policy minimizes sectoral net imports or exports, assuming that distribution policy preserves the existing income distribution, that foreign dissaving is nil, while investment efficiency is unchanged at its 1980-85 level? The problem consists in finding the investment policy which sets sectoral net imports or exports as close to zero as possible during the simulation period.[9]

The outcome of this experiment is also quite somber. The most significant result refers to the degree of attainment of the objective of 'living off our means': in the present stagnant investment environment, it is impossible not only to 'close' the economy, but also to make any noticeable reduction in the existing degree of openness. The degree of economic openness, as measured by the total volume of trade, in the *Living off our means* case is just one per cent less than in the preceding *Status quo and moratorium* case.[10] The explanation of this result is straightforward; when the output response of investment is almost nil, it is nearly impossible to change the composition of output and trade. Investment policy is wholly ineffective as an instrument of policy.[11] Regardless of the size of the changes in investment policy, they do not succeed in modifying performance in productive sectors. Overall growth, as well as growth in most producing sectors, continue to be close to zero. As in the preceding case, and for the same reasons, i.e., positive investment efficiency coefficients, only agriculture, energy and services show positive growth.

This experiment reveals that persistence of a negative environment for investment tends to neutralize efforts to 'live off our means', even if

---

[9] Eq. (27) in Appendix 1 gives a formal definition of the sectoral trade balances. In the notations of Appendix 1, the problem is to find the sequence zg_t of public investment distribution vectors such that $\Sigma_t \, b_t' b_t = \min$. (A comparable formulation is to minimize trade balances in the terminal year.) This type of optimization problem, where both the optimal level and moment of instrument utilization are determined, is also called an optimal control problem. The problem is solved by means of an extension to the nonlinear case of Wolfe's reduced gradient method (Abadie and Carpentier, 1965; see also Abadie, 1978). The algorithm used is due to Lasdon, Waren and Ratner (1980). Lasdon and Waren (1978) or Liebman et al. (1986) describe the algorithm.

[10] See Appendix 3, Table VI.2.

[11] See Appendix 3, Table VI.1.

accompanied by a moratorium on external payments. Underlying trends seem to make the 'open' condition of the Argentine economy more or less unchangeable. It is debatable whether a debt moratorium can be upheld under such circumstances.

Conclusions

In this chapter we have explored an environment characterized by prolongation of adverse trends in the global context, and by continued internal structural opacity and rigidity. A consequence is the inefficiency of structural policy. It does not seem possible to counteract this strong inertia; suspension of foreign debt payments does not modify the situation. In such circumstances, attempts to 'live off our means' do not prosper. Hence, it seems more conducive to increase the clarity and coherence of the economic environment by qualitative and institutional means. Recognition of its dimensions may not overcome the crisis, but may help in enduring it.

6 Fragmentation

Further to the approach adopted in Chapter 5, in this and the following chapter we attempt to inquire about possibilities that are beyond the immediate vicinity. The proximate environment, as we have seen, is comprised of a global crisis that affects economies such as the Argentine with special intensity.

Beyond the immediate setting of the crisis, we find different forms of tension release and process crystallization, as discussed in Chapter 2. All such forms imply dissipation of the instability and ambiguity of the crisis context; they also create and support new growth regimes. In an environment of either fragmentation and economic introversion, or global openness and *détente*, new structuring principles result in definite patterns of configuration for the development process.

Certainty about prevailing structuring modes implies changes in economic behaviour. In the fragmentation case, 'reregulation' takes place at the level of national states. This implies an increase in the self-governing capability of the state, and in its capacity for governance over the general economic environment. This also increases the capacity of the state to manage the resources over which it has direct control, to determine the broad lines of economic evolution and to orient resource utilization in relation to them. In such a context of increased clarity about evolutional patterns, investment activity resumes normal efficiency levels.[1]

Meanwhile, economic introversion may assume different forms. The most elementary implies a nationalistic reaction, where the objectives are national autonomy and self-sufficiency. In a context of financial disruption and general suspension of payments, or of deliberate debt moratorium or repudiation, the economy seeks its maximal capacity to supply and meet internal demands. A more elaborate form of delinking from the international system adds a third component to the developmental focus, i.e., distributive justice.

The closed-unarticulated economy

As in the *Living off our means* scenario in the preceding chapter, the objective in this case is to 'close' the economy as much as possible. This amounts to reducing, to the greatest possible extent, net imports or exports (excess demands or supplies) in all sectors.[2] At the same time, due to suspension of external payments, foreign dissaving is null and overall trade is in balance.

The *closed-unarticulated* economy experiences a remarkable resumption of growth. The cumulative growth rate of total output in the 10-year simulation period is about 8 per cent per year.[3] Given normal conditions of flow and utilization of investable resources, a relatively high internal saving capacity – a savings rate around 20 per cent of national income – results in a relatively high growth rate. When internal savings do not 'flee' abroad and investment efficiency is 'normal', the rate of growth is high.

The recovery of growth capacity enhances the effectiveness of investment policy. It also implies increased structural malleability and a greater capacity for influencing structural change and modifying output and trade structures. Given the 'closure' objective, typically exporting activities such as agriculture and food industries grow much less than the average. Sectors with typically negative trade balances – the industrial sectors in particular – undergo faster-than-average growth. The growth rates of the remaining sectors, comprising

[1] The determination of 'normal' or 'satisfactory' sectoral investment efficiency coefficients used in this and the following chapter is described in Appendix 2.

[2] The mathematical expression for the problem and the method of solution are the same as in the preceding chapter (see Chapter 5, note 8).

[3] See Appendix 3, Table VII.1.

activities which produce mostly nontradables, are faster than average in a situation of excess demand, i.e., the trade sector, and below average in a situation of excess supply, i.e., the remaining sectors.

There are special reasons for the excess demand situation in trading activities. 'Demand' associated with the trade sector actually means the average commercial margin included in the price of different consumption items. The commercialization margins estimated in our demand study – almost one third of the prices of final consumption goods – are larger than the share of trade as a cost factor in the production of output, i.e., in the input-output matrix.[4] Consumption 'demands' directed towards the trade sector are thus larger than the value of commercial 'output'. The disequilibrium reflects the existence of above-average profits and above-average growth potential in the trade sector, as reflected by the experiment.[5]

The investment policy of the *closed-unarticulated* economy is coherent with the evolving structure of production.[6] Among 'secondary' activities, light industry, energy production and heavy industry are stimulated. Among the services sectors, trade and services are promoted, while potentially excess supply sectors, such as finance and transport, are not.

The *closed-unarticulated* strategy is rather successful in 'closing the economy'. As early as the third year, the volume of trade declines by almost one third.[7] This also shows that in spite of the recovered output response to investment and increased effectiveness of policy instruments, autarchy cannot be achieved within the 10-year horizon. If at all possible, economic autarchy seems to be a goal for the very long run.

The evolution of incomes for the different income groups illustrates the 'unarticulated' aspect of the strategy. During the period, income distribution is

---

[4] See Appendix 2.

[5] In this instance, the model simulates the familiar case of market adjustment; the difference is that in the case of the trade sector it is private, not public investment which produces the adjustment. Another possible effect of excess demands in the trade sector is the generation of structural inflation pressures.

[6] See Appendix 3, Table VII.2.

[7] See Appendix 3, Table VII.3. Sectors 6-11 produce mostly nontradables. For these sectors, 'trade balance' refers to excess supply or demand. The 'degree of openness', i.e., the ratio of foreign trade to GNP, decreases from one third to one tenth in the simulation period.

maintained without change at the relatively high initial level of inequality.[8] Thus total income and incomes of different groups grow at the same rate.[9]

The closed-articulated economy

This scenario analyzes the consequences of income redistribution in the context of a strategy of maximal self-sufficiency. It simulates the planning of a *closed-articulated* economy. As in the preceding case, development strategy aims at reducing dependency on imports and exports to a minimum. Moreover, no net capital outflows originate in debt payments, and foreign trade is in balance. But in contrast to the case above, the *closed-articulated* strategy aims at gradually diminishing the degree of income concentration.

As in the *closed-unarticulated* case, the objective of this strategy is to make sectoral trade balances in the different sectors of activity as close to zero as possible.[10] In addition to the objective of economic closedness — to which investment policy is instrumental — this strategy proposes an increase in the degree of socioeconomic articulation, as measured by the evenness of income distribution. The objective of distribution policy is to achieve, at the end of the planning horizon, the degree of distributive equality corresponding to an industrialized economy.[11]

It is interesting to analyze this strategy in comparison with the preceding one. This enables us to study the specific comparative dynamic effects of income redistribution within a process of 'economic closing up'. As we have indicated, the *closed-articulated* case differs from the *closed-unarticulated* case only in its distribution policy.

---

[8] See Appendix 3, Table VII.4. Income distribution in the initial period is seemingly higher than that indicated by the data from 1970 — the latest overall statistics available — on which our study is based (see Appendix 2). That this is so can be deduced from the observed fall in real wages; see e.g. Argentina (1987). As shown by a partial study of income distribution in Buenos Aires in 1974-83 (CEPAL, 1986), the fall in the share of wage income explains the observed increase in income concentration.

[9] When obtaining per capita values, an expected rate of population growth of 1.4 per cent should be taken into account (Argentina, 1986b).

[10] For the mathematical formulation and the solution methods, see Chapter 5, note 8.

[11] The objective is to achieve, in the tenth year, the distributional structure of Spain. Income concentration, as measured by the ratio of the share of the richest 20 per cent to the share of the poorest 20 per cent, is 5.8 in Spain, while in Argentina it is 11.4; see World Bank (1989, Table 30).

distributional equity is valued positively, the *closed-articulated* strategy exhibits superior performance.

Conclusions

In this chapter we have explored the effects of a fragmented *dénouement* of worldwide economic tensions. This form of resolution implies greater certainty and governability in the framework of a closed economy. Two types of adaptations to such an environment were studied. The most elementary form of economic introversion strives towards maximum self-sufficiency, in an environment where foreign payments are suspended. The structural malleability and growth capacity of the economy are high. 'Closedness', however, is not achieved within the planning horizon.

The second form of realization of the closed economy complements autarchy with objectives of social equity. A limited progressive income redistribution is postulated.

Growth in the *closed-articulated* scenario is no less than in the former case. Redistribution may now be understood as the spontaneous effect of high rates of growth and employment in a flexible and democratic political environment. The demand structure of the *closed-articulated* economy is somewhat different from the *unarticulated* case, with higher emphasis on 'basic' goods and services. The degree of 'closedness' achieved is about the same in both cases.

7 Openness

The evolutionary images of this chapter are projected on an international environment which is more symmetric, open and progressive than that of our earlier analysis. The tensions between local, nation-state governing structures, and worldwide techno-productive systems are reconveyed through the gestation of global governing systems. There is no return to closed economies locally controlled according to national criteria, as in the preceding chapter, but an evolution towards an integrated global economy, regulated according to criteria such as global progress and stability.

Regulation on a global scale establishes a context of certainty similar to that which tends to prevail in the modern closed economy. This includes a common body of basic norms, a universal means of payment and free movements of goods, people, technology and capital. The disequilibrating tendencies of the global market are compensated by global structural policies which reorient resource flows.

In this context of increased certainty and stability, investment activity progresses at normal efficiency levels. The strategy of adaptation to global opening consists in exploiting the 'dynamic comparative advantages' of specialization in trade, making collective welfare the strategic focus of structural change.

Global opening may also be considered as a bargaining process of mutual concessions where, for instance, recognition of financial obligations is exchanged for improved trade conditions.

The global opening process may be disturbed by frictions in the gestation of the new global environment, or by inertia in the adaptation of internal structures. Less-than-ideal opening conditions may affect potential welfare growth and limit the dynamic advantages of specialization.

The experiments in this chapter assume a global context of expansion, liberalization and equilibrium in international trade. In this approach, the costs in terms of potential output implied by foreign dissaving may underscore the benefits accruing from the dynamic advantages of specialization.

Another feature of the scenarios in this chapter is the progressive articulation of socioeconomic structures. As in the *closed-articulated* case of the previous chapter, gradual change in the structure of income distribution makes Argentine income distribution in the terminal year similar to that of an industrialized economy. We do not include an 'open-unarticulated' strategy. On the one hand, as discussed in Chapter 2, a collusive-oligopolistic solution of global regulation is unstable; on the other hand, as we have seen in the last section of the preceding chapter, the postulated redistribution does not affect the overall savings and growth performance of the economy.

We now turn to the results of our analysis of these possibilities.

Ideal opening

The first of our experiments with respect to opening and articulation in the economy assumes the absence of trade restrictions. Two other assumptions retained throughout this chapter are an internal relative price structure which somehow conforms to world prices and a nonovervalued domestic currency. All these conditions, of course, are largely fulfilled in the case of global integration described in Chapter 2. *Ideal opening* also assumes the maintenance of a relatively high external trade surplus, at about the same level as in the recent past.[1]

Given certain objectives of income redistribution and a certain level of external trade surplus, effective adaptation to global opening implies allowing

---

[1] The trade surplus in the simulation period is constant, and equal to the average in 1982-85, i.e., 6.65 per cent of national income.

for output and trade structures that ensure the highest attainable welfare. Within a more open and distended economic environment, sectoral self-sufficiency or priority criteria not based on general welfare do not seem rationally justifiable.

The strategic objective is now maximal economic welfare within the 10-year horizon. The role of investment policy is to induce welfare-increasing structural change. Specifically, the problem is to find the investment policy sequence which leads to maximal cumulative welfare during the simulation period, for a given distribution policy over time, and a given rate of external surpluses.[2] The solution to the policy problem is straightforward: it is advantageous to concentrate the development effort in sectors with the highest investment efficiency.[3] According to our study based on international comparison of sectoral investment efficiency, the machinery and equipment sector is the dynamically most advantaged type of activity, with the highest output response to investment.[4] Other studies also seem to suggest the existence of comparative advantages for this type of industrial production in a static sense. On the one hand, there is a relative abundance of highly qualified labour in Argentina, reflected in low wages, unemployment and emigration.[5] On the other hand, industrial branches that produce machinery and equipment are already among the most export-oriented of all industrial branches, i.e., these branches already exhibit a certain degree of specialization in exports.[6]

Within the ideal environment of this experiment, investment policy stimulus is thus concentrated in the machinery sector, that is, the optimal

---

[2] In the notations of Appendix 1, the problem is to find the sequence zg_t of investment policy vectors such that $\Sigma_t W_{t,1}$ = max. A restriction is imposed on the investment policy vector; a minimum of 3 per cent is allocated to all sectors; $zg_t \geq [0.03, 0.03, ..., 0.03]'$. That is, the maximal feasible sectoral share is 70 per cent. The method of solution is the same as in earlier chapters (see Chapter 5, note 8).

[3] Let us recall that output structure does not affect income distribution, as uniform distribution is assumed across sectors (see Appendix 2).

[4] Statistical estimation and selection of marginal output capital coefficients are documented in Appendix 2.

[5] According to Llach (1988), comparative advantage based in the relative abundance of skilled labour has probably increased in the 1980s, as suggested by international comparison of wage levels.

[6] Aspiazu, Bisang and Kosakoff (1988, p. 31) emphasize '[...] the existence of relatively high export coefficients in some manufacturing sectors, activities in which Argentina has developed a number of comparative advantages, particularly in production of short and flexible series with a high content of skilled labour. Among these activities there are various types of industrial machinery and apparatuses, both mechanical and electrical, professional and scientific equipment, etc.'

investment policy associated with maximal welfare growth allocates maximum admissible effort to the machinery sector.[7]

As discussed in Chapter 3, the notion of investment should be understood in a very broad sense. Investment policy should be conceived of primarily as technological and educational policies oriented towards fostering industrial innovation and technological creation and diffusion.

Capacity for creation and adaptation of technology cannot be thoroughly enhanced unless the public sector is transformed. General organizational change aimed at making the entire state apparatus more instrumental and receptive to technical change implies some kind of intangible investment. More tangible forms of public investments are those which create 'overhead social capital' for advanced industrial activities. These include investments in infrastructure for research, education and communication, which in turn create important 'external economies' for knowledge- and information-intensive production.[8]

In this framework, even expenditures commonly understood as consumption expenditures – e.g. current expenditures in education and health – should be regarded as investments, to the extent that they promote productivity and upgrade skill levels.

The notion of public investment also covers all forms of subsidization (tax exemptions, subsidized credit, etc.), and direct investment in publicly owned or mixed enterprises. Even the additional costs due to tariffs and other means of protecting domestic production should be seen as an investment, justified by an expected flow of discounted social benefits of a larger order of magnitude.

---

[7] See Appendix 3, Table IX.2.

[8] In the present age of 'global technology', these types of policies are considered relevant even for advanced industrial economies. Cf. the following conclusion in a study by the US Academy of Engineering (Lee and Reid, 1991, pp. 76-7):

> The government must take action on many fronts to strengthen the foundations of the US technical enterprise — the nation's work force, its social capital (i.e., educational system and public infrastructure), as well as its fiscal and regulatory environment. Above all, state and federal policymakers must work together with corporate and academic leaders to develop a broad national consensus regarding the need to improve technology development, adoption, adaptation, and diffusion throughout the US industrial economy. This consensus, in concert with other national policies, can provide the necessary impetus, coherence, and operational guidelines for the many diverse private and public policy actions required to meet the challenges of globalization.

Openness, in the ideal circumstances sketched here, gives rise to spectacular growth in both overall and machinery output. Machinery production, for example, grows three time faster than the average.[9]

The possibility of full realization of dynamic comparative advantages drastically changes the structure of foreign trade. Specialization in agricultural and agroindustrial exports vanishes rapidly: in the terminal year, Argentina becomes a net importer of agriculture-based products (agriculture and food).[10] The volume of agricultural exports is approximately constant, while the trade balance of food industries becomes negative in the middle of the 10-year period. Imports of foodstuffs surpass agricultural exports by the end of the period.

Industrial activities are subjected to the opposite phenomenon. After having been a net importer, the economy becomes a net exporter of manufactures. At the end of the period, intensive exploitation of dynamic comparative advantages leads the economy towards almost complete specialization in exports of machinery and equipment. Such exports then become almost three times larger than other imports of manufactures. On the whole, the economy undergoes an intense process of 'export substitution' during the period, due to the rapid expansion of industrial exports.

In the *Ideal opening* case, rapid growth allows for a relatively high rate of external debt servicing. Formerly a debtor internationally, the Argentine economy becomes a net creditor towards the end of the period (i.e., in the seventh year).

The structural evolution of employment directly reflects the profound changes which occur in the composition of output. The most notable changes are (a) the share of manufacturing jobs is almost tripled, (b) employment in tertiary sectors falls, from about one half to one third of total employment, (c) the share of employees in agriculture-based activities is reduced by one third, (d) average labour productivity increases, due to the change in output structure in favour of activities, such as machinery production, that are less labour intensive.[11]

Even if *Ideal opening* is not a particularly labour-intensive strategy, its rate of growth in employment is higher than the expected growth in labour

---

[9] Total output grows at 11.7 per cent per year during the simulation period; see Appendix 3, Table IX.1. Such high and sustained growth rates and rapid structural change can only be compared, in the past few decades, to those of the newly industrialized Asian economies.

[10] See Appendix 3, Table IX.3. Recall that for sectors producing mainly nontradables, net imports or exports refer to excess demand or excess supply situations.

[11] See Appendix 3, Table IX.4.

supply.[12] As in some of the other strategies, this may lead to gradual absorption of un- and underemployment, an increase in labour-force participation rates and to excess demand pressures.

Ideal opening postulates a process of progressive income redistribution aimed at attaining the distributional structure of an advanced economy by the terminal year.[13] Changes in income shares are compatible with increases in income for all groups, that is, redistribution may be perceived as a 'Pareto sanctioned' policy.[14]

Although a result of policies specifically oriented towards reducing inequalities, the redistribution in *Ideal opening* may be seen, in the same way as that of the *closed-articulated* economy, as a spontaneous process resulting from rapid economic growth. In effect, the income trajectory of *Ideal opening* reaches the level of an industrial economy before the terminal year.[15]

Let us now characterize the effects of *Ideal opening* on income levels and distribution in somewhat more detail. Welfare indicators associated with this strategy reveal its relatively egalitarian features: the democratic index grows more than average income (per employed person) and the efficiency-equity index rises more than national income. This strategy is comparatively more favourable to low income groups — the poverty-weighted index grows faster than the democratic index.

Quid pro quo

Ideal opening may also be understood as the result of a process of negotiating dynamic economic interdependence or as a *quid pro quo* fostering global progress. The level of trade surpluses and the rate of foreign debt servicing may be regarded as counterparts to the degree and type of participation attributed to Argentina in the international economic system. *Ideal opening* assumed elimination of all kinds of trade barriers, normal conditions in the global financial environment and fluent connections with global technological systems. Openness thus assumes that economic interlocutors — in particular, external creditors – give some degree of consideration to the debtors' interests

[12] The expected growth in labour supply is 1.8 per cent per year (Argentina, 1986b).

[13] As in the preceding *closed-articulated* case, the income distribution structure in the tenth year is the same as Spain's (see Chapter 6, note 14).

[14] See Appendix 3, Table IX.5.

[15] At the implied rate of per capita income growth (8.2 per cent per year), in ten years Argentina would surpass the level of Spain in 1985 (estimated from data in World Bank, 1987, Table 1).

and needs, thereby implying a certain acceptance of the debtors' well-being among the creditors' objectives.

Similarly, the right to participate on an equal footing in an open, interdependent and progressive international framework has, as counterparts, the establishment of stable rules of economic functioning and a certain level of recognition of financial obligations. This means recognizing the interests of economic interlocutors as arguments of the own welfare function.

We now intend to analyze formally the effects of such a merger of economic interests. The new objective function, representing the *quid pro quos* of negotiated global opening, has two arguments. The first reflects internal welfare; the second represents the flow of resources which augment the welfare of foreign creditors. While the possibility of maximizing internal welfare depends on the possibility of reaping the dynamic advantages of international specialization, the outward flow of resources depends on the rate of foreign trade surplus. The relative importance accorded to internal and external welfare is reflected by their respective weights in the welfare function.[16] In a first experiment, domestic welfare is given a weight of two thirds (and foreign welfare the remaining third). As in the preceding case the economy rapidly tends to specialize in machinery production.[17] But, as a consequence of the resulting high 'optimal' level of foreign dissaving associated with these weights, the rate of growth decreases considerably.[18] This type of opening does not seem auspicious, as the resulting growth rate does not differ from the closed economy cases.

When the weight of foreign welfare in the objective function is reduced to one tenth, the 'optimal' coefficient of external dissaving is lower, less than that corresponding to the *Ideal opening* case.[19] The implicit renunciation of internal welfare implied by *Ideal opening* – and *a fortiori* by that verified in 1982-85 – would be somewhere within the interval 1/10 - 2/3.

---

16 In the notations of Appendix 1, the problem consists in determining the coefficient ω of external dissaving and the investment policy sequence zg_t that maximize the objective $\Sigma_t\ (W_{t,1})^{\xi}\ (\varphi)^{1-\xi}$, where $W_{t,1}$ denotes national income, φ foreign dissaving, and ξ the weight of internal welfare in the welfare function.

17 See Appendix 3, Table IX.1a.

18 The resulting coefficient of foreign dissaving is 10.4 per cent.

19 The dissaving coefficient which results from this second experiment with $\xi = 0.9$ is 3.1 per cent. Recall that the coefficient of *Ideal opening* was 6.65 per cent, the average for 1982-85.

More realism?

The economic landscapes configured in the preceding section may seem illusory. The unimpeded and smooth absorption of the accelerating flow of Argentine industrial exports by world markets as well as the capacity of the domestic economy to generate them can be questioned. Rates of export growth such as those implied by *Ideal opening* were infrequent during the world trade boom prior to 1980, and more so since then.[20]

In future evolutionary prospects of a more open and articulated economy, there may then be more realism in assuming limits to export expansion. For some reason or other, either internal (e.g. supply inertia) or external (e.g. trade restrictions), export growth cannot exceed a certain level.

More realism? aims at the same strategic objective as *Ideal opening*, that is, to maximize the welfare of society along the period, assuming the same rate of external debt servicing and the same income redistribution policy. It differs only in the fact that a 'realistic' limit is set on export growth; total exports cannot grow by more than 10 per cent per year.[21]

The solution shows that obstacles or limits to export expansion have significant effects on the growth possibilities of the economy and on the type of structural changes that it is able to undergo. When the 'dynamic comparative advantages' that result from specializing in activities with high expansion potential cannot be exploited unrestrainedly, the overall rate of economic growth is substantially reduced.[22] The rate is still high, however, and implies relatively intense use of the dynamic advantages of specialization.

Machinery is no longer the sector where most of the growth effort occurs. This sector grows at a high rate, particularly in the first years of the period, but it is eventually surpassed by agriculture, which grows at high rates throughout the period. Among goods-producing activities, light industry and construction also enjoy 'comparative dynamic advantages', that is, their growth is above the average.

---

[20] The rate of export growth in *Ideal opening* is 17.7 per cent per year. Among non-oil-exporting economies, such a rate has only been attained, in 1965-80, by South Korea (27.2 per cent); no country approached it during the period 1980-89 (World Bank, 1991, Table 14).

[21] The formal expression of the problem is the same as in note 2, where the restriction $\iota' q_t \leq 1.1\ \iota' q_{t-1}$ replaces the restriction on investment policy $zg_t \geq [0.03, 0.03, ..., 0.03]'$. The method of solution is the same as in the preceding sections (see Chapter 5, note 8).

[22] It declines by more than one third, from 11.7 to 7.2 per cent per year during the period. See Appendix 3, Tables IX.1 and X.1.

When there is a ceiling on export growth, the time-pattern of welfare-maximizing investment policy is quite different from that of the *Ideal opening* investment policy, which concentrated on machinery production. *More realism?* implies a rather 'counterintuitive' investment policy, as it is characterized by considerable emphasis on agriculture, larger than indicated by its relative expansion rate.[23] This result probably depends on the combined effect of two different factors: (a) the relatively high initial participation of agriculture in exports, that is, the fact that agriculture is an established export activity, and (b) the relatively lower output response of agricultural investment, which implies a relatively high additional capital requirement per additional unit of output.

The *More realism?* solution would then suggest that when there are restrictions on export expansion, the pre-existing 'static comparative advantage' aspects which favour agriculture offset the longer run 'dynamic comparative advantage' aspects, which favour activities such as machinery and equipment production.

Public investment in the agricultural sector — once again emphasized here — should be widely understood as formation of human and physical productive capacities and capabilities. The notion thus encompasses the creation of social overhead in infrastructures that directly or indirectly benefit rural areas. It also includes investment in productive knowledge. This less tangible type of investment embraces, first, the generation of knowledge, i.e., investment in basic research in biology and related sciences, and its applications (biotechnology). It also embraces market-oriented research in product innovation, and in prospecting and penetration of new markets.[24] Equally important is even and effective diffusion of research results (agricultural extension) and the upgrading of skills (education, professional formation). Lastly, and in symmetry with the case of industrial protection, the comprehensive notion of public investment should also include the reduction or elimination of export taxes or differential exchange rates applied to agriculture and 'traditional' exports.

[23] The share of agriculture averages somewhat more than one third; see Appendix 3, Table X.2.

[24] Product differentiation and innovation may partially offset the tendency towards declining terms of trade for agricultural products and foodstuffs.

The outcome represented by rapid agricultural expansion considerably increases the degree of specialization in agricultural exports.[25] Light and heavy industry continue to be net importers all along the period. The machinery sector, however, becomes a net exporter towards the middle of the period; during the first half the rapid increase in output replaces imports, satisfying a growing domestic demand, while in the second half it allows for rapid export expansion.

These results concerning dynamic comparative advantages in the Argentine economy are in accordance with those of other studies based on qualitative and inductive methods. These studies also emphasize the importance of intensively applying knowledge and information to the advancement of agriculture and the machinery and equipment industries.[26]

A lower rate of growth in total output and exports in *More realism?* as compared to *Ideal opening* implies a lower capacity for excess saving and creation of a trade surplus, and consequently, a lower rate of decrease in external debt. The difference, however, is not remarkable: the external position turns positive in the eighth year, one year later than in the former case.

At first glance, the changes in employment structure do not seem to contribute to a more realistic vision of possible structural change. The expansion of agricultural output is accompanied by substantial employment growth in that sector.[27] This expansion, however, should be viewed in the context of the contemporary technical revolution. New communication and information systems, modern forms of production and new lifestyles gradually blur the sharp contrasts of the rural/urban dichotomy.

Employment contracts in some sectors. The strongest reduction in employment shares, by one half, is in the services sector. This sector includes most of the self-employed, whose numbers increased dramatically in the stagnant environment of the 1980s.

In spite of differences in the patterns of structural change in employment, both 'ideal' and 'realistic' strategies have similar effects on total employment; the higher labour intensity in the latter compensates the higher growth in the former.

In *More realism?* the socioeconomic articulation process, which aims at achieving the distributional structure of an industrialized economy, takes

[25] See Appendix 3, Table X.3.
[26] See Ferrer (1987) and the *Okita Report* (ACIJ, 1987).
[27] See Appendix 3, Table X.4.

place in an environment of relatively slower growth. The resulting redistribution is 'non-Paretian', as there is a slight decline in average incomes of high income groups.[28] Distribution policy should then require a higher degree of intentionality and caution.

Conclusions

We have analysed the consequences of an adaptation of governing structures in response to environmental pressures from globalized techno-productive systems. A global *polis* stabilizes a transition towards a more open and symmetric international system, by means of norms and policies inspired in universal welfare principles. In an ideal form of evolution in this type of context, the Argentine economy adapts optimally, intensively exploiting the dynamic comparative advantages of industrial specialization. The economy develops rapidly, while maintaining a high level of trade surplus, and distributive equity is progressively augmented. The adaptational problem may also be understood as a bargaining process where seemingly divergent interests are recognized by the participants as their own. There are, of course, limits to such recognition, beyond which openness does not convey advantages.

If the evolving global integration were prevented by internal or external factors which restrict the expansion of Argentine exports, the resulting rate of growth would be lower and the changes in productive structure less encompassing. The pattern of dynamic comparative advantage maintains some 'traditional' traits, combining a high share of agricultural exports with growing specialization in machinery production.

[28] See Appendix 3, Table X.5.

PART III
EPILOGUE

8 Gestation

The world economy has been in a state of crisis for more than a decade. A period of intense and continuous change has affected the very basis of all production systems and their global forms of articulation. New methods and techniques, new functions and products have permeated all fields of human activity – disrupting and unravelling existing, established organizational forms. The huge stock of knowledge accumulated by basic science during the last decades has been brought to its critical mass by the economic cycle and scattered, in a multitude of combinations, over all conceivable fields of application. This is the background of contemporary economic turbulence. The strong volatility indicated by economic barometers reflects rapid transformation in relational structures and behaviour.

At the level of perception, the general uncertainty and changeability of expectations reflect the same phenomena of rapid structural change and relative erosion of established modes of comprehension and prediction. At the level of sociopolitical organization and policy, the global technological revolution has largely eroded the instruments of traditional, nationally based economic policy - imposing a return to *laissez faire*, quite independently of ideological inclinations. The state is in crisis, and the crisis is not merely fiscal.

This description corresponds to a juncture of instability of the global economic system. It seems to traverse a region where small variations in external conditions may provoke far-reaching changes in the evolutionary regime. In this region, outside the immediate vicinity of a point, evolutionary trajectories are not uniquely given. Outside this immediate, deterministic vicinity, there are potential bifurcations in the evolutionary regime, which represent different configurative modes of the global system.

The central evolutionary mechanism is given by the tension between two aspects of the system: the techno-productive apparatus and regulatory mechanisms. As bearers of technological advances, productive systems expand with increasing effectiveness on a global scale, thereby eroding existing regulatory systems, based mainly on the nation-state form of social organization. Weakened policy instruments add to the opacity of the economic structure.

In the absence of global regulatory mechanisms, disequilibria originating from oligopolistic interaction within the techno-productive system tend to accumulate. Growing financial and monetary disequilibria and expanding protectionism reflect increasing tensions in oligopolistic competition. Above a certain level, accumulated tensions are released and reabsorbed by the gestation of a systemic transformation.

Two main types of systemic change can be distinguished. In the first type, tensions in the system bring about collapse and fragmentation of the global techno-productive system. Once the nongovernability threshold is attained, the system ruptures. The new systems which result are relatively closed, determinate and regulable. Nation-states, possibly forming economic blocs or zones, are the new regulating units.

Within these new, regulated systems, techno-productive structures expand in an orderly fashion, and the different parts of the new, fragmented global system regain growth momentum. In this relatively autonomous evolutionary regime, the economic system may be guided by the objective of maximal expansion and self-sufficiency. A dualistic techno-productive system arises, with large differences in productivity between strategic firms and production in general, subordination of the working force to production objectives, low wages and a concentrated distribution structure. The politico-ideological cement of this evolutionary pattern is nationalism, which has a unifying effect as a form of cult of the collective identity of the fragmentary system.

In another kind of fragmentation, the principle of the welfare of its members guides the system in its search for self-sufficiency. Production systems are permeated more evenly by technological revolution; techniques favour autonomous expansion of individual creative powers and allow for influence on roles and results in the work process. Distribution of the social product tends to level out.

Tensions accumulated by the global system may be resolved by a second type of systemic change, symmetric to those described above. In this case, the potential of tension acts as a morphogenic attractor. A global regulatory system develops, capable of reorienting and stabilizing worldwide deployment of the techno-productive system.

One form of realization of global governance is directly connected to the expansionary requirements of the techno-productive system. Noncooperative solutions of the oligopolistic game imply high risks of disruption. These risks may be reduced by collusive coordination by the participants in order to maximize surplus and growth. This global oligarchy accentuates the existing dualistic pattern of technology utilization and resource allocation on a global scale, where rapid technological progress takes place in the centers and low absorption and growth in the peripheries. Increasing polarization makes this type of realization unstable.

The gestation of a global *polis* is the most advanced form of systemic mutation. The global *polis* emerges as a representative space for articulating universal interests and aspirations. The natural governing principle for the global *polis* is human welfare. Resource flows are regulated so as to compensate for the disequilibrating, dualistic tendencies of the global techno-productive system. Global expansion objectives are thus combined with global distributive equity.

Status quo is an intermediate form of evolution. It represents a prolongation of the current situation. Disequilibria persist without attaining the mutation threshold, in an environment of global stagnation and deep crisis in less industrialized economies. Agreements regarding global opening are extended, along with informal protectionism. Ambitious attempts to achieve macroeconomic coordination coexist with noncooperative policies. Recurrent proposals for solving the problem of foreign debt are accompanied by continuous drains on the resources of indebted countries.

Such are the main features of the evolutionary alternatives for the external environment of the Argentine economy. Rather, they may be regarded as representing alternatives of the general environment to which each particular economy now belongs and whose evolution it tends to follow. Evolution in this sense is overdeterminate, and separate evolutions are necessarily congruent with each other and with the general pattern. Each action or transformation has a conscious aspect, however, which is also congruent with the general pattern. Our study may be understood as an exploration of internal policy responses or adaptations to different configurations of the global situation. Or, our study may be viewed as an attempt to determine the most efficient sequence of structural policy decisions which fulfil given internal ends, within a given time horizon, in a given global environment.

The possibility space described above in terms of general configurations has been explored in detail in the case of the Argentine economy. A theoretical sonde, a model of the economy, performs the operations which replicate the stages traversed by the economy in different configurations. The principle of construction is the greatest possible simplicity compatible with analysis of concrete policy alternatives. The analytical framework distinguishes among sectors of activity and income classes, and among the fundamental components of the economic process (production, consumption, investment, etc.). In particular, structural policy instruments are defined which guide the economy through various evolutionary landscapes. The main features of the strategies are summarized and compared in Table 8.1.

An essential difference in the alternative configurations for the future of the Argentine economy is given by whether or not global tensions are resolved according to some of the suggested means. In several intermediate scenarios, global uncertainties and their internal effects remain. Ambiguities in the global context are reflected internally by low investment productivity. Productive potential is dissipated in an environment where incoherent anticipations or mutually inconsistent plans cancel each other out.

The *open-unarticulated* economy is characterized by a stagflation environment. If past policies are retained in this environment, the result is continued stagnation, with small differences between sectors – although the situation is slightly better in agriculture. The pattern of relations with the world economy remains unchanged.

Table 8.1: Comparison of strategies (exponential growth rates in the simulation period)

	Foreign dissaving[a]	Gini coef.	Income	Welfare[b]	Openness[c]
Open-unarticulated	6.6	0.0	0.3	0.3	7.7
Unilateral moratorium	0.0	0.0	0.2	0.2	6.8
'Living off our means'	0.0	0.0	0.2	0.2	0.0
Closed-unarticulated	0.0	0.0	8.4	8.4	-16.8
Closed-articulated	0.0	-2.5	8.4	10.1	-16.8
Ideal opening	6.6	-2.5	9.6	11.4	6.7
Quid pro quo	10.4	-2.5	6.8	8.5	5.4
More realism?	6.6	-2.5	6.7	8.4	0.4

[a] Rate of trade surplus as a per cent of national income (*not* rate of change in this case); constant throughout the period. [b] *Efficiency-equity* index, i.e., (one minus) the Gini coefficient times GNP. [c] Degree of openness defined as the ratio of total trade to total output. *Source*: Appendix 3.

The stagnating environment is very resilient, and does not respond to economic policy changes. A *unilateral moratorium* on external debt payments, for instance, does not perceptibly modify the situation. The considerable increase in investment potential thus achieved is — as in the past – dissipated. The evolution of the economy is very similar to that of the status quo situation.

Under these circumstances, the economy exhibits very low flexibility. The same difficulties are confronted when an attempt is made to close the economy, '*living off our means*' after external debt is repudiated. Investment effectiveness is so low that even when resources are concentrated in sectors with the highest import-substitution potential, the specialization pattern of the economy remains almost unchanged. The degree of openness of the economy and its dependency on imports and exports are not modified. A durable moratorium on debt may not seem viable under such conditions.

The above intermediate scenarios give rise to particularly negative results for the Argentine economy, to a large extent due to the fragility of internal structuring mechanisms. Lacking its own evolutionary regime, the economy is highly vulnerable to a turbulent environment.

The situation is quite different in the scenarios where uncertainty is resolved. In any mode of global restructuring, the Argentine economy recovers its dynamism and structural malleability. Crisis resolution results in a decrease in global uncertainty and its effects, i.e., high international interest rates and tendencies towards capital 'flight'. Evolutionary trends in the economy become more discernible; there is more certainty and stability in plans and expectations. Stagflation is replaced by new growth regimes which, in different ways, establish environments with greater predictability and efficiency in investment activity, and increased clarity and consistency in the norms and conduct of economic regulation.

International disruption implies a generalized economic retreat. General suspension of payments is followed by fragmentation of the international monetary system and, as a consequence, financial and exchange controls are reintroduced. The real counterpart of financial disruption is the collapse of world trade and the reappearance of administered trade and trade barriers.

One type of fragmentation emerges as a sharp national reaction. Strategic efforts are focused wholly on national power and sufficiency. Maximal tension in the economy implies suppression of other, nonfunctional objectives and aspirations. The sociopolitical organizational mode congruent with this type of economic structuring is some form (despotic, consensual) of autocracy. Structural policy is oriented exclusively towards productive self-sufficiency; dependency on industrial imports or agricultural exports is minimized. Equity or welfare criteria do not intervene in policy formation.

The growth rate related to this type of *closed-unarticulated* economy is high. It is comparable to other periods of intense growth in Argentina. Growth is the consequence of normal levels of investment efficiency accompanied by a high capacity to generate internal surpluses. There is now responsiveness to structural policy instruments. Investment policy succeeds in guiding the economy towards higher degrees of self-sufficiency. However, even after 10 years of maximal concentration on the internal market, the economy maintains a certain degree of openness.

Another type of fragmentation results in an evolutionary regime where autonomy, self-sufficiency and equity criteria are equally important. Financial collapse eliminates one of the most visible forms of dependency, i.e., external debt. Capital flight is thus curtailed, or even reversed, to the extent that it can run a blockade or evade confiscation by external creditors. The response to the collapse of international trade is a policy of productive self-sufficiency oriented towards meeting internal needs. The objective of distribution policy is to increase equality, as a reflection of uniform diffusion of technology, knowledge and initiative.

In spite of gradual income redistribution, growth in this *closed-articulated* economic regime is not less than in the more dualistic unarticulated economy. Accumulation behaviour is such that high investable resources are generated even when, as in this case, income concentration gradually diminishes to attain the level of an industrialized country. The flexibility and regulability regained by the economy permit a rapid decrease in import and export dependency, which does not disappear totally, however. As compared to the unarticulated strategy, this strategy is centered more on production of goods and services demanded by low income groups.

By gestation of the global *polis*, disruptive forces are channelled and reabsorbed through progressive institutional mutation towards increased interdependency, equality and *détente*. This seems to be the central evolutionary trend of this *fin de siècle*: adaptation of regulatory systems congruent with the universal character of existing production, communication and exchange technologies. In relation to this central historical trend, other evolutionary forms appear as more or less transient modes resulting from disturbances in the adjustment process. In this context, not only status quo forms of global stagnation and turbulence, but also the different types of international fragmentation become transient.

The central tendency is towards world economic openness within the framework of steadfast norms of collective coexistence. An integrated economic system unfolds on a world scale, with its own fiscal and monetary regulatory mechanisms. Based on the sovereignty of the global *polis*, a common monetary system ensures fluid exchanges, stability in valuations, and investment flows in accordance with international profitability curves. Global fiscal policy tends to dynamize the global economy and to equate living conditions.

Concepts such as 'country risk' and problems such as 'capital flight' lose their substance in this context. The economic environment acquires greater stability and predictability; the productive efficiency of created capacities tends to be normalized.

The most effective dynamic adjustment to this generally open environment involves orienting structural change towards the greatest attainable welfare. Sectoral self-sufficiency or priority criteria not based on an increase in general welfare have no justification in an open, predictable environment. This strategy tends to specialize in dynamically more efficient activities, i.e., with long run, dynamic comparative advantages, rather than in activities which are advantageous in international cost comparisons at a given point in time.

In one ideal form of adaptation to global openness, internal supplies expand frictionlessly and external demand absorbs Argentine exports without obstacles. This *ideal opening* tends to concentrate strategic efforts on the dynamically most efficient sector — machinery and equipment — and the resulting growth is very high. Structural policy devotes an important resource share to this sector, and increased private investment flows into it. The pattern of specialization in the economy changes over time in favour of machinery output. Formerly a large net importer, the machinery sector gradually becomes an important net exporter. The relative weight of agricultural exports tends to decline.

As a result of the swift pace of industrialization, there is rapid change in the employment structure, detrimental mainly to 'informal' jobs in the service sectors. The progressive income redistribution which characterizes this strategy may be regarded as a spontaneous outcome of a high growth environment.

In the framework of general openness, discontinuation of capital flight and normalized investment efficiency, the high accumulative capacity of the economy simultaneously gives rise to a high rate of growth and a high rate of external surpluses. The latter reduces external debt and then finances exports and foreign investments.

Ideal opening may also be understood as the result of a bargaining process, with mutual concessions among the participants, or a *quid pro quo* which favours global progress. Concession represents — at least partial – recognition of the interlocutor's perspective. This implies that the interlocutor's interests are to some degree included among one's own interests. In terms of welfare functions, this implies extending the standard notion of welfare – normally restricted to some national boundary – so as to include the welfare of other participants.

The problem of external debt illustrates this intermingling of interests. The creditor is interested in repayment of the debt, the debtor in growth. When the creditor recognizes the debtor's interests, barriers to growth (protectionism, incentives for 'capital flight', etc.) may be eliminated in favour of conditions which stimulate development (technology transfer, direct investment, etc.). When the debtor acknowledges the creditor's interests, the resource flow which increases the creditor's welfare (debt service) is incorporated into his own welfare function. The extent of such mutual recognition is obviously limited. In a case which could be regarded as maximal renunciation to the debtor's welfare (where the weight of internal welfare is two thirds, while debt servicing accounts for the remaining third), welfare growth does not notably differ from the closed-economy cases.

The last openness case occurs under nonideal conditions, in a setting of relative opaqueness in international relations or inflexibility in internal structure, where dynamic advantages of specialization cannot be fully exploited. It emerges in an environment where, although principal uncertainties and disequilibrating factors have been removed, international trade conditions are not completely transparent or the redeployment capacity of the internal production structure faces certain limitations (restrictions are characterized as yearly export growth of no more than 10 per cent).

More realism? regarding the possibility that advanced participation in the world economy will confront some level of friction in internal or external adjustment, results in limits to growth and welfare. Welfare growth is not greater than in the closed economy cases. But the growth potential obtained through specialization in the *More realism?* case is higher; a high savings rate allows external debt to be cancelled in the medium term and external assets to be accumulated in the long run.

The evolving economic structure now has two driving forces where agriculture and machinery production appear as the dynamically most efficient activities. In these two sectors, structural policy concentrates a large share of resources on basic research, technology, human resource development, construction and modernization of infrastructure, and direct investment. The specialization pattern of the economy changes, with machinery exports gradually established as a parallel to agricultural exports. The employment structure evolves in the same direction. As compared to *Ideal opening* growth is now lower, which suggests a higher degree of intent in the social articulation process represented by the redistribution policy of this strategy.

PART IV
APPENDICES

1 Model

GENERAL NOTATIONS

k	denotes the number of income groups
n	denotes the number of producing sectors
$\hat{}$	above a vector transforms it into a diagonal matrix
$'$	denotes transposition
ι	is the summing vector (1, 1, ..., 1)'
I	is the unit matrix.

POLICY PARAMETERS

V^p_t	(k x n) matrix of sectoral value added coefficients, private
z^g_t	(n x 1) vector of sectoral allocation of sectoral allocation of public investment.

BEHAVIOURAL PARAMETERS

V^d	(1 x n) matrix of sectoral direct tax coefficients
V^i	(1 x n) matrix of sectoral indirect taxes
V^g	(1 x n) matrix of sectoral value added distribution coefficients, government
χ	(scalar) share of wages in total fiscal revenues
θ^p	(n x k) matrix of subsistence consumption parameters, private
Γ^p	(n x k) matrix of marginal propensities to consume, private
Γ^g	(n x 1) matrix of incremental capital output ratios
α	(n x n) matrix (diagonal) of incremental capital output ratios
i	(scalar) rate of interest on the external debt

B — $(n \times n)$ distribution matrix of investment demands
A — $(n \times n)$ matrix of technical coefficients
M — $(n \times n)$ distribution matrix for imports of inputs
Π — $(n \times n)$ matrix (diagonal) of input import coefficients by sector of destination)
N — $(n \times n)$ distribution matrix of imports of investment goods
σ — $(n \times n)$ matrix (diagonal) of import content coefficients of investment demands
Λ — $(k \times n)$ matrix of labour productivity ratios
r — $(n \times n)$ matrix (diagonal) of exponential rates of productivity change.

WEIGHTING PARAMETERS

ν_i — $(i=1,2,\ldots,k)$ 'poverty weights' of the social welfare function.

EXOGENOUS VARIABLES

ω_t — (scalar) foreign savings as a proportion of national income
$\bar{q}_t$ — $(n \times 1)$ vector of exogenous exports
$\bar{m}_t$ — $(n \times 1)$ vector of exogenous imports.

ENDOGENOUS VARIABLES

x_t — $(n \times 1)$ vector of gross outputs
$y^p{}_t$ — $(k \times 1)$ vector of disposable incomes
$y^g{}_t$ — (scalar) income of the government
$c^p{}_t$ — $(n \times 1)$ vector of consumption expenditures, private
$c^g{}_t$ — $(n \times 1)$ vector of consumption expenditures, government
c_t — $(n \times 1)$ vector of consumption expenditures, total
$s^p{}_t$ — $(k \times 1)$ vector of savings by income class, private
$s^g{}_t$ — (scalar) government savings
φ_t — (scalar) foreign saving
u_t — (scalar) adds foreign saving to domestic saving
$s^p{}_t{}^*$ — (scalar) total (domestic plus foreign) saving, private
$d^p{}_t$ — $(n \times 1)$ vector of investments by sector of destination, private
$z^p{}_t$ — $(n \times 1)$ vector of sectoral allocation of investment, private
$s^g{}_t{}^*$ — (scalar) total (domestic plus foreign) savings, government
$d^g{}_t$ — $(n \times 1)$ vector of public investment by sector of destination
d_t — $(n \times 1)$ vector of total investment by sector of destination
f_t — $(n \times 1)$ vector of investment demands by sector of origin
δ_t — $(n \times 1)$ vector of excess demands
$m^a{}_t$ — $(n \times 1)$ vector of imports of intermediate inputs by sector of origin
$f^m{}_t$ — $(n \times 1)$ vector of imports of investment goods by sector of origin
$\hat{m}_t$ — $(n \times 1)$ vector of total noncompetitive imports by sector of origin
q_t — $(n \times 1)$ vector of total exports
m_t — $(n \times 1)$ vector of total imports
$\bar{y}^p{}_t$ — $(k \times 1)$ vector of average incomes.

STATE VARIABLES

$W_{1,t}$	(scalar) national income
$W_{2,t}$	(scalar) democratic index
$W_{3,t}$	(scalar) poverty weighted index
$W_{4,t}$	(scalar) 'efficiency-equity' index
$Gini_t$	(scalar) coefficient of inequality
E_t	(scalar) external indebtedness
b_t	(n x 1) vector of sectoral trade balances
l_t	(k x 1) vector of labour requirements by income class
λ_t	(n x 1) vector of sectoral labour requirements.

DYNAMIC CORE EQUATIONS

Private incomes

$$y^p_t = V^p_t\, x_t \tag{1}$$

Government incomes

$$y^g_t = V^g\, x_t \tag{2}$$

Sectoral private consumption

$$c^p_t = \theta^p\, \iota + \Gamma^p\, y^p_t \tag{3}$$

Sectoral government consumption

$$c^g_t = \Gamma^g\, y^g_t \tag{4}$$

Private saving by income class

$$s^p_t = -\theta^p\, '\iota + (I - \iota'\, \Gamma^p)\, y^p_t \tag{5}$$

Government savings

$$s^g_t = (1 - \iota'\, \Gamma^g)\, y^g_t \tag{6}$$

External debt growth

$$E_{t+1} = E_t\,(1 + i\,) + \varphi_t \tag{7}$$

Total (domestic plus foreign) private savings

$$s^p_t{}^* = \iota'\, s^p_t\,(1 + u_t) \tag{8}$$

Total (domestic plus foreign) government savings

$$s^g_t{}^* = s^g_t\,(1 + u_t) \tag{9}$$

Private investment allocation vector

$$z^p_t = \frac{\alpha\,(x_t - 0.5\,x_{t-1} - 0.3\,x_{t-2} - 0.2\,x_{t-3})}{\iota'\alpha\,(x_t - 0.5\,x_{t-1} - 0.3\,x_{t-2} - 0.2\,x_{t-3})} \tag{10}$$

Private investments by sector of destination

$$d^p_t = z^p_t\, s^p_t{}^* \tag{11}$$

Public investment by sector of destination

$$d^g_t = z^g_t\, s^g_t{}^* \tag{12}$$

Total investments by sector of destination

$$d_t = d^p_t + d^g_t \tag{13}$$

Output growth

$$x_{t+1} = \alpha^{-1}\, d_t + x_t \tag{14}$$

IDENTITIES AND PERIPHERAL EQUATIONS

Total fiscal revenues

$$g_t = (V^d + V^i)\, x_t \tag{15}$$

Income of the government

$$y^g_t = (1 - \chi)\, g_t \qquad (16)$$

Value added by the government

$$V^g = (1 - \chi)(V^d + V^i) \qquad (17)$$

Foreign saving

$$\varphi_t = \omega_t\, \iota'\, y^p_t \qquad (18)$$

Rate of foreign saving

$$u_t = \frac{\varphi_t}{\iota' s^p_t + s^g_t} \qquad (19)$$

Total investments by sector of origin

$$f_t = B\, d_t \qquad (20)$$

Imports of intermediate inputs by sector of origin (noncompetitive)

$$m^a_t = M\, \Pi\, x_t \qquad (21)$$

Imports of investment goods by sector of origin (noncompetitive)

$$f^m_t = N\, \sigma\, d_t \qquad (22)$$

Total noncompetitive import demands by sector of origin

$$\tilde{m}_t = m^a_t + f^m_t + \bar{m}_t \qquad (23)$$

Excess demands

$$\delta_t = x_t - Ax_t - c_t - f_t - \bar{q}_t - \tilde{m}_t \qquad (24)$$

Total sectoral exports

$$q_t = \delta_t + \bar{q}_t \text{ (for } \delta_i \geq 0,\ i = 1, 2, ..., n) \qquad (25)$$

Total sectoral imports

$$m_t = -\delta_t + \bar{m}_t \text{ (for } \delta_i < 0,\ i = 1, 2, ..., n) \qquad (26)$$

Sectoral balance of trade

$$b_t = x_t - Ax_t - c_t - f_t \qquad (27)$$

Employment by income class

$$l_t = \Lambda_0\, e^{-rt}\, x_t \qquad (28)$$

Sectoral employment

$$\lambda_t = \widehat{\Lambda'_0 \iota}\ e^{-rt}\, x_t \qquad (29)$$

National income

$$W_{1,t} = \iota'\, y^p_t \qquad (30)$$

Democratic index

$$W_{2,t} = (y_{t,1} \cdot y_{t,2} \cdot \ldots \cdot y_{t,k})^{1/k} \qquad (31)$$

Poverty weighted index

$$W_{3,t} = y^{v1}_{t,1} \cdot y^{v2}_{t,2} \cdot \ldots \cdot y^{vk}_{t,k} \qquad (32)$$

'Efficiency-equity' index

$$W_{4,t} = W_{1,t}\,(1 - Gini_t) \qquad (33)$$

Gini coefficient of inequality

$$Gini_t = 1 + 1/k + 2\,(\bar{y}^p_{t,1} + 2\,\bar{y}^p_{t,2} + \ldots + k\,\bar{y}^p_{t,k})(k\, \iota'\, y^p_t)^{-1} \qquad (34)$$

Average incomes

$$\bar{y}^p_t = \widehat{l^{-1}_t}\ y^p_t \qquad (35)$$

2 Estimation

This appendix comprises the sources and methods of empirical implementation of the model described mathematically in Appendix 1. We document the estimation of (a) parameters of functions describing the behaviour of the economy, (b) initial values of endogenous variables (sectoral gross outputs and external debt), and (c) values of exogenous variables (dissaving coefficients, exogenous imports and exports). Given (a), (b) and (c), and the sequence of policy instrument values (investment and distribution policies), the model is solved recursively forward in time. The result is a *simulation* of the temporal evolution of the economy.

Policy variables can be stipulated exogenously – as in the historical simulation — or obtained from optimization of an objective function.

Technical coefficients and gross outputs

The matrix A of technical coefficients depicts the interindustrial structure of the economy, and establishes a link between intermediate (input) demands and gross outputs. The A matrix intervenes in the determination of sectoral excess demands; eq. (24) in Appendix 1.

Our 11-sectors A matrix is obtained by aggregating a 56-sectors matrix, constructed with census data from 1973 (Argentina, 1986c).

Initial sectoral gross outputs are obtained from our aggregated 11-sectors matrix, actualizing the 1973 values by the index of variation in sectoral outputs in Argentina (1986a).

Income distribution

Income distribution functions relate incomes to sectoral gross outputs; eqs. (1) and (2) in Appendix 1.

Private incomes

The matrix of private incomes has as many rows as there are income groups, and as many columns as producing sectors. It shows the shares of sectoral gross outputs accruing to each income group as income net of taxes. These coefficients are treated as policy instruments in some simulations. In the historical simulations and the distributional status quo scenario (the *closed-unarticulated* case), distribution coefficients adopt their actual values. Information on income distribution in Argentina is fragmentary and not up-to-date. We adopt the most recent values (1970) given by an international source (World Bank, 1989, Table 30). Three income classes are defined: *High, Middle* and *Low*, corresponding to 20, 60 and 20 percent of households respectively, in decreasing order of income. The source does not distinguish among sectors of activity.

The matrix of private incomes distributes sectoral disposable value added among income groups. That is, it distributes the value of each sector's output not attributed to intermediate inputs or tax payments. Formally:

$$V^p = \begin{bmatrix} 0.503 \\ 0.453 \\ 0.044 \end{bmatrix} . \; [\, \iota' - \iota' A - (1 - \chi)(V^d + V^i) \,]$$

In other words, value added in each sector is assumed to be distributed among *High, Middle* and *Low* income groups according to the same proportions.

Government income

The matrix of government incomes determines the value added at the government's disposal, once wage payments by the government – accounted for as private incomes – have been deducted from government revenues; eqs. (15)-(17) in Appendix 1. This matrix is constant over all simulations, that is, distributive policies do not affect the government's income share. The variables χ , V^d and V^i intervene in the construction of this matrix. The corresponding values are:

$\chi = 0.5$

V^d = [0.0036 0.0004 0.0006 0.0001 0.0002 0.0004 0.0001 0.0028 0.0005 0.0062 0.0082]

V^i = [0.0009 0.0266 0.0390 0.0081 0.0151 0.0109 0.0269 0.0512 0.0097 0.0026 0.0060]

Sources: Internal Revenue Service (DGI), National Institute of Statistics (INDEC) and National Budget 1985.

Consumption functions

Consumption by different income groups (and the government) of goods and services from producing sectors is derived from an extended linear expenditure system (Lluch, 1973), where exogenous, fixed prices are assumed.

Private consumption

Private consumption functions, eq. (3) in Appendix 1, comprise a matrix of constants (often interpreted as subsistence consumptions), and a matrix of linear coefficients (marginal propensities). They are estimated by ordinary minimum squares from original data in the household expenditure survey (*Encuesta de Gasto de los Hogares*) from the National Institute of Statistics (INDEC). The survey encompasses 2,349 households during seven months in 1985.

The values of subsistence consumptions are reproduced below (in 1970 *australes*), after having been blown up to account for the entire population. Spontaneous annual growth in subsistence consumptions of 1 per cent is assumed.

$$\theta p_{85} = \begin{bmatrix} 100.7 & 37.52 & 2.7 \\ 356.2 & 110.5 & 103.3 \\ -23.4 & -18.8 & 45.5 \\ 2.6 & 2.6 & 4.5 \\ -159.2 & -13.0 & 14.9 \\ 0.0 & 0.0 & 0.0 \\ 29.2 & -18.2 & 16.9 \\ 16.9 & 17.5 & 84.5 \\ 55.9 & 7.1 & 14.4 \\ -2.6 & -2.6 & 0.4 \\ -308.1 & -51.3 & 29.9 \end{bmatrix}$$

The matrix of marginal consumption propensities by income group is as follows:

$$\Gamma p = \begin{bmatrix} 0.0066 & 0.0258 & 0.0361 \\ 0.0348 & 0.1219 & 0.0986 \\ 0.1371 & 0.1375 & 0.0522 \\ 0.0052 & 0.0063 & 0.0010 \\ 0.0580 & 0.0169 & 0.0239 \\ 0.0 & 0.0 & 0.0 \\ 0.0358 & 0.0535 & 0.0084 \\ 0.1727 & 0.1817 & 0.0812 \\ 0.0082 & 0.0256 & 0.0117 \\ 0.0043 & 0.0039 & 0.0010 \\ 0.2280 & 0.1538 & 0.0585 \end{bmatrix}$$

Government consumption

Quantities of consumption goods and services demanded by the government are linear homogeneous functions of government income; there are no 'subsistence consumptions' for the government. Consumption propensities are constant in all simulations, that is, no change is assumed in the savings/investment behaviour of the government:

Γ^g = [0.0 0.0328 0.0316 0.0318 0.0 0.0 0.0677 0.0 0.0688 0.0 0.0403]'.

Sources: National Budget 1985 and original data (on the sectoral composition of government expenditure) from *Contaduría General de la Nación*.

Investment coefficients

Two types of investment coefficients are used in the model. The first links, for each sector, additions in productive capacities to additions in gross outputs. These incremental capital output ratios are defined by eq. (14) in Appendix 1; their inverses are referred to as 'investment efficiency coefficients'. The second type of investment coefficient reflects the composition by sector of origin of sectoral investments (sector of destination), that is, it transforms sectoral investments into investment demands; eq. (20). The historical values of the investment policies dealt with in Chapter 4 are also documented here.

Investment efficiency

The sectoral incremental capital output ratios are defined as the slopes of linear functions which relate capital goods to gross outputs in each sector of activity. Estimation of these coefficients thus requires data over a series of years on capital stock installed in each sector. There is no official information on capital stocks or investments in Argentina. The strategy in this study was to construct a sample of corporations based on the *Encuesta de Sociedades Anónimas* (INDEC), and to assemble the data from published balance sheets. For each sector – with the exception of transport and services – the (deflated) values of fixed capital assets for the period 1975-85 are set in relation to the sales values. For transport and services – with no corporations in the INDEC sample – the sources are, respectively, (a) balance sheets of public transport enterprises, and (b) public investment in services production. As shown in the table below, in most cases the (least squares) adjustment is not satisfactory.

The values adopted in our non-status-quo investment scenarios in Chapters 6 and 7 are composed of (a) positive coefficients obtained by regression from the Argentine sample whose R^2 is higher than 0.5, and (b) the 'worst' (highest) sectoral coefficient among those for Mexico (Buzaglo, 1984, p. 222) and South Korea (Dervis, de Melo and Robinson, 1982, p. 116). To our knowledge, these are the only recent estimations of sectoral capital output ratios.

Matrix α **:** Incremental capital output ratios

	Argentina				South	Value
	Sample	R^2	**Coeff.**	**Mexico**	**Korea**	**adopted**
Agriculture	2	0.79	1.12	1.94	1.20	1.12
Food processing	12	0.0	0.0	0.59	0.19	0.59
Light industry	41	0.56	1.10	0.78	0.35	1.10
Heavy industry	9	0.95	1.73	1.38	0.54	1.73
Machinery	10	0.70	-0.2	0.52	0.19	0.52
Construction	3	0.30	0.25	0.41	1.50	1.50
Energy	5	0.07	0.70	3.15	0.42	3.15
Trade	10	0.06	-0.04	0.28	n.d.	1.40
Transport	-	0.14	2.15	6.0	n.d.	6.0
Finance	6	0.37	-0.05	0.37	n.d.	1.40
Services	-	0.02	0.01	2.62	1.40	2.62

Note: n.d. sectors corresponding to South Korea are approximated by the value for the service sector.

Origin and destination of investments

Matrix B in eq. (20) shows how a unit investment is decomposed in each sector into goods and services originating in the different sectors, that is, it allows us to determine the sectoral origin of investments realized in each sector. The data source is the same as in the preceding subsection, with the exception of Energy and Finance, where the sources are now, respectively, (a) balance sheets of public energy enterprises, and (b) the Central Bank of Argentina.

The proportions in the sectoral 'investment baskets' are determined from the composition of fixed capital goods in the balance sheets.

Matrix *B*: Composition (by sector of origin) of investments (by sector of destination)

Sector	1	2	3	4	5	6	7	8	9	10	11
1 Agriculture	0.0273						0.0001		0.0157		
2 Food processing											
3 Light industry	0.4032	0.0322	0.1543	0.0019	0.2690	0.0503	0.4751	0.1706	0.1365	0.1354	0.1175
4 Heavy industry									0.2322		
5 Machinery	0.3098	0.4944	0.6563	0.7422	0.4847	0.7318	0.4163	0.0384	0.3472	0.0640	0.2555
6 Construction	0.2597	0.4734	0.1894	0.2559	0.2463	0.2179	0.1085	0.7910	0.2684	0.8006	0.6270
7 Energy											
8 Trade											
9 Transport											
10 Finance											
11 Services											

Distribution of public investment

Investment policy vectors used in the historical simulations reported in Chapter 4 and in the initial conditions for the remaining simulations are based on the national budgets for corresponding years.

Foreign trade and debt

In addition to sectoral excess demands, the separate determination of sectoral imports and exports requires information on 'noncompetitive' imports and exports; eqs. (25) and (26) in Appendix 1.

Noncompetitive imports

These are composed of (a) demands for intermediate inputs, (b) demands for investment goods, and (c) 'exogenous imports'.

Imports of inputs are represented by a (diagonal) matrix of coefficients of contents of imported inputs by sector of destination, and a matrix of distribution by origin of input imports by destination; eq. (21) in Appendix 1. Both are constructed by aggregation from Argentina (1986c).

Imports of investment goods are based on sectoral investment (by sector of destination), which has a known imported content, given by a diagonal matrix of coefficients. Decomposition by sector of origin is given by a distribution matrix; equation (22).

There are no data on sectoral investments in Argentina, but there is a detailed study on capital imports (Lifschitz and Liachovitzky, 1986). The following coefficients are derived from simulated values of sectoral investments (Simulation IV) and historical values of imports of investment goods in Lifschitz and Liachovitzky (1986):

$$\sigma = [0.13 \quad 0.03 \quad 0.34 \quad 0.07 \quad 0.56 \quad 0.03 \quad 0.01 \quad 0.07 \quad 0.01 \quad 0.02 \quad 0.01]$$

The *N* matrix of distribution of imported capital goods is obtained by aggregation of the matrix presented in Lifschitz and Liachovitzky (1986).

'Exogenous imports' are imports of nonproducible goods corresponding to typically net exporting sectors (tropical foods in this case). The values adopted are in 1970 *australes*; they represent average imports in 1980-85 and are assumed to grow at 2 per cent per year:

$$\bar{m}_{85} = [4.0 \quad 4.0 \quad 0.0 \quad 0.0 \quad 0.0 \quad 0.0 \quad 0.0 \quad 0.0 \quad 0.0 \quad 0.0 \quad 0.0]'$$

Source: INDEC (*Anuario de Comercio Exterior* and *Estadística Mensual,* various issues).

Noncompetitive exports

Exports by typically net importing sectors, mainly industrial sectors, are given in 1970 *australes*, represent the average for 1980-85 and are assumed to grow by 2 per cent per year:

$$\bar{q}_{85} = [0.0 \quad 0.0 \quad 22.0 \quad 29.0 \quad 17.0 \quad 0.0 \quad 18.0 \quad 0.0 \quad 0.0 \quad 0.0 \quad 0.0]'$$

Source: Ibid.

External debt and savings

Foreign dissaving in the model is an exogenously determined proportion of national income; eq. (18) in Appendix 1. In some of the historical simulations, the 'actual' value from national accounts (Argentina, 1986a) is used.

In each period, external debt – whose initial value is known – grows as an effect of the interest rate, and increases or decreases by the addition or subtraction of trade deficits or surpluses; eq. (7). According to Central Bank estimations, the value of the debt (in 1983) was 1,646 1970 *australes*, and the average interest rate was 8.5 per cent. These are our adopted values.

Employment coefficients

Employment associated with different strategies over time is determined by means of a matrix of average labour productivity ratios, by activity sector and income group, annually adjusted by a diagonal matrix of exponential rates of productivity change; eqs. (28) and (29) of Appendix 1.

Average productivity

Due to the absence of data on income distribution at the sectoral level, uniform sectoral productivities are assumed. Thus, uniform proportions are applied to the sectoral employed per produced 1970 *austral.*

$$\Lambda_{80} = \begin{bmatrix} 0.2 \\ 0.6 \\ 0.2 \end{bmatrix} . [\,708.3 \quad 167.4 \quad 338.0 \quad 761.6 \quad 166.3 \quad 698.5 \quad 101.1 \quad 788.8 \quad 233.8 \quad 315.2 \quad 1280.2\,]$$

Sources: Employment, Argentina (1983); output, Argentina (1986a).

Productivity growth

Rates of change in labour productivity result of comparing two points in time, 1970 and 1980. The sectoral values are not satisfactory (there are several negative rates) and criticism may be directed towards the quality of the Census of 1970. The overall rate of change, 1.16 per cent per year, is adopted for all sectors. This is perhaps not satisfactory either, as underemployement and 'disguised unemployment' have probably increased during the period. *Sources*: Argentina (1977, 1983, and 1985b).

Welfare functions

Four different types of welfare functions were defined: (a) national income, (b) the democratic index, (c) the poverty weighted index, and (d) the efficiency-equity index. Functions (a) and (d) are simple arithmetic transformations of endogenous variables in the model; eqs. (30) and (33) in Appendix 1.

Democratic index: This is represented by a harmonic average of individual incomes; eq. (31). In this case, instead of individuals, we have income groups with different respective populations. Average incomes of each group are weighted by their relative population; *High* 0.2, *Middle* 0.6 and *Low* 0.2.

Poverty weighted index: In this index, lower income groups are given an exogenous, higher weight, as expressed in eq. (32). Our weights are *High* 0.0, *Middle* 0.6 and *Low* 0.4.

3 Simulations

Simulation V

TABLE V.1 GROSS OUTPUTS

	AUSTRALES OF 1970							ANNUAL GROWTH RATES (PERCENT)							
SECTOR	YEAR 0	YEAR 1	YEAR 2	YEAR 3	YEAR 4	YEAR 5	YEAR 10	1/0	2/1	3/2	4/3	5/4	5/0	10/5	10/0
AGRICULTURE	1889	1890	1890	1891	1892	1897	1917	0.0	0.0	0.1	0.0	0.3	0.1	0.2	0.1
FOOD PROCESSING	2089	2089	2089	2089	2089	2089	2089	0.0	0.0	0.0	0.0	0.0	0.0	0.0	0.0
LIGHT INDUSTRY	1981	1981	1981	1981	1981	1981	1981	0.0	0.0	0.0	0.0	0.0	0.0	0.0	0.0
HEAVY INDUSTRY	660	660	660	660	660	660	660	0.0	0.0	0.0	0.0	0.0	0.0	0.0	0.0
MACHINERY	894	783	695	689	601	474	243	-12.4	-11.3	-0.8	-12.8	-21.2	-11.9	-12.5	-12.2
CONSTRUCTION	735	735	735	735	735	735	735	0.0	0.0	0.0	0.0	0.0	0.0	0.0	0.0
ENERGY	1651	1684	1722	1760	1822	1891	2310	2.0	2.3	2.2	3.5	3.8	2.8	4.1	3.4
TRADE	1653	1653	1653	1653	1653	1653	1653	0.0	0.0	0.0	0.0	0.0	0.0	0.0	0.0
TRANSPORT	1898	1898	1898	1898	1898	1898	1898	0.0	0.0	0.0	0.0	0.0	0.0	0.0	0.0
FINANCE	963	963	963	963	963	963	963	0.0	0.0	0.0	0.0	0.0	0.0	0.0	0.0
SERVICES	2023	2048	2072	2097	2137	2182	2697	1.2	1.2	1.2	1.9	2.1	1.5	1.9	1.7
TOTAL	16437	16384	16358	16417	16431	16424	16846	-0.3	-0.2	0.4	0.1	0.0	0.0	0.5	0.2

TABLE V.2 IMPORTS, EXPORTS, BALANCE OF TRADE, EXTERNAL DEBT
AUSTRALES OF 1970

SECTOR		YEAR 0	YEAR 1	YEAR 2	YEAR 3	YEAR 4	YEAR 5	YEAR 10
AGRICULTURE	IMPORTS	36	36	36	36	36	36	37
	EXPORTS	565	558	560	538	526	517	472
	B. T.	529	522	524	502	490	480	435
FOOD PROCESSING	IMPORTS	5	5	5	5	5	5	5
	EXPORTS	463	445	425	402	379	356	217
	B. T.	458	440	420	397	374	351	212
LIGHT INDUSTRY	IMPORTS	977	1007	1048	1056	1079	1095	878
	EXPORTS	22	22	23	23	24	24	27
	B. T.	-955	-985	-1025	-1033	-1055	-1069	-851
HEAVY INDUSTRY	IMPORTS	154	151	149	149	147	144	138
	EXPORTS	200	249	432	245	216	176	158
	B. T.	46	98	283	96	69	63	20
MACHINERY	IMPORTS	1521	1678	2907	1701	1529	1400	667
	EXPORTS	17	17	18	18	18	19	21
	B. T.	-1504	-1661	-2889	-1683	-1511	-1381	-646
CONSTRUCTION	IMPORTS	0.0	0.0	0.0	0.0	0.0	0.0	0.0
	EXPORTS	742	857	1921	956	813	692	552
	B. T.	742	857	1921	956	813	692	552
ENERGY	IMPORTS	51	52	52	52	53	54	58
	EXPORTS	651	675	703	729	777	852	1161
	B. T.	600	623	651	676	723	779	1103
TRADE	IMPORTS	1781	1777	1778	1800	1810	1815	1947
	EXPORTS	0.0	0.0	0.0	0.0	0.0	0.0	0.0
	B. T.	-1781	-1777	-1778	-1800	-1810	-1815	-1947
TRANSPORT	IMPORTS	36	36	36	36	36	36	36
	EXPORTS	878	876	870	859	851	846	781
	B. T.	842	839	834	823	815	810	744
FINANCE	IMPORTS	7	7	7	7	7	7	7
	EXPORTS	655	649	642	635	628	620	579
	B. T.	648	642	635	628	621	614	572
SERVICES	IMPORTS	4	4	4	4	4	4	4
	EXPORTS	380	405	427	443	474	512	644
	B. T.	376	401	423	438	470	508	640
TOTAL	IMPORTS	4574	4754	6023	4847	4706	4594	3778
	EXPORTS	4574	4754	6023	4847	4706	4594	4611
	B. T.	0.0	0.0	0.0	0.0	0.0	0.0	833
EXTERNAL DEBT		3360	3763	4215	4721	5287	5921	10435

Simulation VI

TABLE VI.1 GROSS OUTPUTS

	AUSTRALES OF 1970							ANNUAL GROWTH RATES (PERCENT)							
SECTOR	YEAR 0	YEAR 1	YEAR 2	YEAR 3	YEAR 4	YEAR 5	YEAR 10	1/0	2/1	3/2	4/3	5/4	5/0	10/5	10/0
AGRICULTURE	1889	1943	1995	1995	2007	2015	2177	2.9	2.6	0.0	0.6	0.4	1.3	1.6	1.4
FOOD PROCESSING	2089	2089	2089	2089	2089	2089	2089	0.0	0.0	0.0	0.0	0.0	0.0	0.0	0.0
LIGHT INDUSTRY	1981	1981	1981	1981	1981	1981	1981	0.0	0.0	0.0	0.0	0.0	0.0	0.0	0.0
HEAVY INDUSTRY	660	660	660	660	660	660	660	0.0	0.0	0.0	0.0	0.0	0.0	0.0	0.0
MACHINERY	894	894	894	894	894	894	98	0.0	0.0	0.0	0.0	0.0	0.0	-35.8	-19.9
CONSTRUCTION	735	735	735	735	735	735	735	0.0	0.0	0.0	0.0	0.0	0.0	0.0	0.0
ENERGY	1651	1675	1704	1731	1767	1800	2058	1.4	1.7	1.6	2.1	1.8	1.7	2.7	2.2
TRADE	1653	1653	1653	1653	1653	1653	1653	0.0	0.0	0.0	0.0	0.0	0.0	0.0	0.0
TRANSPORT	1898	1898	1898	1898	1898	1898	1898	0.0	0.0	0.0	0.0	0.0	0.0	0.0	0.0
FINANCE	963	963	963	963	963	963	963	0.0	0.0	0.0	0.0	0.0	0.0	0.0	0.0
SERVICES	2023	2054	2083	2107	2157	2198	2501	1.5	1.4	1.2	2.4	1.9	1.7	2.6	2.1
TOTAL	16437	16545	16655	16706	16805	16886	16812	0.7	0.7	0.3	0.6	0.5	0.5	-0.1	0.2

TABLE VI.2 IMPORTS, EXPORTS, BALANCE OF TRADE, EXTERNAL DEBT
AUSTRALES OF 1970

SECTOR		YEAR 0	YEAR 1	YEAR 2	YEAR 3	YEAR 4	YEAR 5	YEAR 10
AGRICULTURE	IMPORTS	36	36	36	36	36	37	37
	EXPORTS	564	608	657	632	629	625	719
	B. T.	528	572	621	596	592	588	682
FOOD PROCESSING	IMPORTS	5	5	5	5	5	5	5
	EXPORTS	463	437	410	388	362	337	209
	B. T.	458	432	405	383	357	332	203
LIGHT INDUSTRY	IMPORTS	971	1018	1073	1026	1018	1045	862
	EXPORTS	22	22	23	23	24	24	27
	B. T.	-949	-996	-1050	-1003	-994	-1021	-835
HEAVY INDUSTRY	IMPORTS	154	154	154	155	155	155	135
	EXPORTS	206	250	395	190	127	130	158
	B. T.	52	95	240	36	-27	-25	23
MACHINERY	IMPORTS	1471	1583	2802	1546	1324	1137	845
	EXPORTS	17	17	18	18	18	19	21
	B. T.	-1454	-1565	-2784	-1528	-1305	-1119	-825
CONSTRUCTION	IMPORTS	0.0	0.0	0.0	0.0	0.0	0.0	0.0
	EXPORTS	680	811	1894	902	760	628	613
	B. T.	680	811	1894	902	760	628	613
ENERGY	IMPORTS	51	52	52	52	53	53	56
	EXPORTS	651	661	675	690	711	729	918
	B. T.	600	609	623	638	659	677	863
TRADE	IMPORTS	1781	1818	1854	1874	1905	1931	1963
	EXPORTS	0.0	0.0	0.0	0.0	0.0	0.0	0.0
	B. T.	-1781	-1818	-1854	-1874	-1905	-1931	-1963
TRANSPORT	IMPORTS	36	36	36	36	36	36	36
	EXPORTS	878	864	850	839	825	813	788
	B. T.	842	828	814	803	789	777	752
FINANCE	IMPORTS	7	7	8	8	8	8	6
	EXPORTS	655	648	640	633	625	617	579
	B. T.	648	640	633	625	617	610	572
SERVICES	IMPORTS	4	4	4	4	4	4	4
	EXPORTS	380	396	410	426	460	489	751
	B. T.	376	392	406	422	456	484	747
TOTAL	IMPORTS	4517	4713	6024	4742	4543	4411	3951
	EXPORTS	4517	4713	6024	4742	4543	4411	4783
	B. T.	0.0	0.0	0.0	0.0	0.0	0.0	832
EXTERNAL DEBT		3360	3763	4215	4721	5287	5921	10436

Simulation VII

TABLE VII.1 GROSS OUTPUTS
AUSTRALES OF 1970

SECTOR	YEAR 0	YEAR 1	YEAR 2	YEAR 3	YEAR 4	YEAR 5	YEAR 10	1/0	2/1	3/2	4/3	5/4	5/0	10/5	10/0
								ANNUAL GROWTH RATES (PERCENT)							
AGRICULTURE	1889	1945	1977	2001	2022	2038	2208	3.0	1.6	1.2	1.0	0.8	1.5	1.6	1.6
FOOD PROCESSING	2089	1920	1798	1844	1823	1814	3147	-8.1	-6.3	2.5	-1.1	-0.5	-2.8	1.6	4.2
LIGHT INDUSTRY	1981	2834	3556	4174	4770	5225	7222	43.1	25.5	17.4	14.3	9.6	21.4	6.7	13.8
HEAVY INDUSTRY	660	750	858	931	1085	1184	1851	13.5	14.5	8.5	16.5	9.1	12.4	9.3	10.9
MACHINERY	894	1405	1768	2056	2294	2480	3206	57.1	25.8	16.3	11.5	8.1	22.6	5.3	13.6
CONSTRUCTION	735	999	1203	1370	1504	1610	2095	35.8	20.5	13.9	9.8	7.1	17.0	5.4	11.0
ENERGY	1651	1547	1498	1481	1523	1533	2134	-6.3	-3.2	-1.1	2.9	0.6	-1.5	6.8	2.6
TRADE	1653	2021	2540	3255	3870	4475	7859	22.3	25.7	28.1	18.9	15.6	22.0	11.9	16.9
TRANSPORT	1898	1946	1968	1990	2036	2069	2352	2.5	1.2	1.1	2.3	1.6	1.7	2.6	2.2
FINANCE	963	1038	1094	1139	1175	1204	1366	7.7	5.5	4.1	3.2	2.5	4.6	2.6	3.6
SERVICES	2023	1959	1988	2025	2078	2411	4079	-3.2	1.5	1.8	2.6	16.0	3.6	11.1	7.3
TOTAL	16437	18363	20249	22266	24180	26044	37518	11.7	10.3	10.0	8.6	7.7	9.4	7.6	8.6

TABLE VII.2 PUBLIC INVESTMENT BY DESTINATION
AUSTRALES OF 1970

SECTOR	YEAR 0		YEAR 1		YEAR 2		YEAR 3		YEAR 4		YEAR 5		YEAR 10	
AGRICULTURE	0.0	0.0	0.0	0.0	0.0	0.0	0.0	0.0	0.0	0.0	0.0	0.0	155	8.9
FOOD PROCESSING	24	3.0	0.0	0.0	88	9.4	0.0	0.0	0.0	0.0	0.0	0.0	129	7.4
LIGHT INDUSTRY	109	13.9	158	18.4	89	9.4	130	12.7	28	2.5	89	7.4	72	4.1
HEAVY INDUSTRY	81	10.3	79	9.1	0.0	0.0	162	15.8	21	1.8	60	5.0	64	3.7
MACHINERY	96	12.2	0.0	0.0	0.0	0.0	0.0	0.0	0.0	0.0	0.0	0.0	54	3.1
CONSTRUCTION	0.0	0.0	18	2.1	0.0	0.0	0.0	0.0	0.0	0.0	0.0	0.0	308	17.6
ENERGY	0.0	0.0	97	11.3	107	11.4	215	21.0	0.0	0.0	231	19.2	302	17.2
TRADE	237	30.2	347	40.4	527	56.2	252	24.6	229	20.5	234	19.4	224	12.8
TRANSPORT	0.0	0.0	0.0	0.0	39	4.2	168	16.4	47	4.2	211	17.5	100	5.7
FINANCE	0.0	0.0	0.0	0.0	0.0	0.0	0.0	0.0	0.0	0.0	0.0	0.0	131	7.5
SERVICES	238	30.3	161	18.7	89	9.5	98	9.6	789	70.9	380	31.5	212	12.1
TOTAL	785	100.0	859	100.0	939	100.0	1027	100.0	1113	100.0	1205	100.0	1752	100.0

TABLE VII.3 IMPORTS, EXPORTS, BALANCE OF TRADE, EXTERNAL DEBT
AUSTRALES OF 1970

SECTOR		YEAR 0	YEAR 1	YEAR 2	YEAR 3	YEAR 4	YEAR 5	YEAR 10
AGRICULTURE	IMPORTS	36	36	36	38	39	40	109
	EXPORTS	559	632	662	615	598	570	0
	B. T.	523	596	627	578	559	530	-109
FOOD PROCESSING	IMPORTS	5	5	8	83	213	339	7
	EXPORTS	463	212	0.0	0.0	0.0	0.0	186
	B. T.	458	207	-8	-83	-213	-339	179
LIGHT INDUSTRY	IMPORTS	806	488	267	225	254	277	382
	EXPORTS	22	22	23	97	328	322	88
	B. T.	-784	-466	-245	-129	74	45	-294
HEAVY INDUSTRY	IMPORTS	154	197	236	266	304	331	477
	EXPORTS	138	123	117	59	135	119	402
	B. T.	-17	-74	-119	-207	-168	-212	-75
MACHINERY	IMPORTS	852	407	118	135	150	162	210
	EXPORTS	17	17	51	98	346	349	50
	B. T.	-835	-389	-67	-38	196	187	-159
CONSTRUCTION	IMPORTS	30	0.0	0.0	0.0	1	0.0	0.0
	EXPORTS	0.0	6	0.0	206	0.0	123	63
	B. T.	-30	6	0.0	206	-1	123	63
ENERGY	IMPORTS	51	53	55	57	62	64	100
	EXPORTS	651	461	321	204	145	51	22
	B. T.	600	408	266	147	84	-14	-78
TRADE	IMPORTS	1781	1837	1725	1436	1225	1011	11
	EXPORTS	0.0	0.0	0.0	0.0	0.0	0.0	62
	B. T.	-1781	-1837	-1725	-1436	-1225	-1011	51
TRANSPORT	IMPORTS	36	38	39	40	42	44	219
	EXPORTS	878	784	666	536	439	343	0.0
	B. T.	842	746	627	496	397	299	-219
FINANCE	IMPORTS	7	9	11	13	15	17	26
	EXPORTS	655	694	718	730	736	734	721
	B. T.	648	685	707	717	721	717	695
SERVICES	IMPORTS	4	5	63	252	423	326	55
	EXPORTS	380	122	0.0	0.0	0.0	0.0	0.0
	B. T.	376	117	-63	-252	-423	-326	-55
TOTAL	IMPORTS	3763	3074	2559	2545	2728	2611	1595
	EXPORTS	3763	3074	2559	2545	2728	2611	1595
	B. T.	0.0	0.0	0.0	0.0	0.0	0.0	0.0
EXTERNAL DEBT		5376	6021	6744	7553	8459	9474	16697

TABLE VII.4 INCOME BY INCOME GROUP
AUSTRALES OF 1970

INCOME GROUP	YEAR 0		YEAR 1		YEAR 2		YEAR 3		YEAR 4		YEAR 5		YEAR 10	
HIGH	4392	50.3	4806	50.3	5254	50.3	5747	50.3	6230	50.3	6745	50.3	9805	50.3
MIDDLE	3955	45.3	4328	45.3	4732	45.3	5176	45.3	5611	45.3	6074	45.3	8830	45.3
LOW	384	4.4	420	4.4	460	4.4	503	4.4	545	4.4	590	4.4	858	4.4
TOTAL	8732	100.0	9555	100.0	10446	100.0	11426	100.0	12385	100.0	13409	100.0	19493	100.0
GINI COEFFICIENT		0.438		0.438		0.438		0.438		0.438		0.438		0.438

Simulation VIII

TABLE VIII.1 GROSS OUTPUTS
AUSTRALES OF 1970

ANNUAL GROWTH RATES (PERCENT)

SECTOR	YEAR 0	YEAR 1	YEAR 2	YEAR 3	YEAR 4	YEAR 5	YEAR 10	1/0	2/1	3/2	4/3	5/4	5/0	10/5	10/0
AGRICULTURE	1889	1945	1979	2003	2026	2043	2247	3.0	1.7	1.3	1.1	0.8	1.6	1.9	1.7
FOOD PROCESSING	2089	1936	1824	1878	1864	1860	3322	-7.3	-5.8	2.9	-0.7	-0.2	-2.3	12.3	4.7
LIGHT INDUSTRY	1981	2835	3567	4201	4799	5266	7145	43.1	25.8	17.8	14.2	9.7	21.6	6.3	13.7
HEAVY INDUSTRY	660	749	857	933	1086	1189	1830	13.5	14.4	8.8	16.4	9.5	12.5	9.0	10.7
MACHINERY	894	1355	1687	1960	2184	2360	3006	51.6	24.5	16.2	11.5	8.1	21.4	5.0	12.9
CONSTRUCTION	735	999	1198	1370	1508	1616	2030	35.8	20.0	14.4	10.0	7.2	17.1	4.7	10.7
ENERGY	1651	1547	1498	1479	1520	1529	2156	-6.3	-3.2	-1.3	2.8	0.6	-1.5	7.1	2.7
TRADE	1653	2026	2584	3341	3991	4636	8093	22.6	27.5	29.3	19.4	16.2	22.9	11.8	17.2
TRANSPORT	1898	1946	1969	1995	2045	2089	2413	2.5	1.2	1.3	2.5	2.1	1.9	2.9	2.4
FINANCE	963	1038	1096	1144	1183	1214	1399	7.7	5.7	4.4	3.4	2.6	4.7	2.9	3.8
SERVICES	2023	1962	1989	2022	2079	2387	3913	-3.0	1.4	1.6	2.8	14.8	3.4	10.4	6.8
TOTAL	16437	18339	20249	22326	24284	26188	37555	11.6	10.4	10.3	8.8	7.8	9.8	7.5	8.6

TABLE VIII.2 PUBLIC INVESTMENT BY DESTINATION
AUSTRALES OF 1970

SECTOR	YEAR 0		YEAR 1		YEAR 2		YEAR 3		YEAR 4		YEAR 5		YEAR 10	
AGRICULTURE	0.0	0.0	0.0	0.0	0.0	0.0	0.0	0.0	0.0	0.0	19	1.5	148	8.4
FOOD PROCESSING	33	4.2	0.0	0.0	90	9.6	0.0	0.0	0.0	0.0	0.0	0.0	144	8.2
LIGHT INDUSTRY	110	14.0	146	17.0	73	7.8	113	11.0	32	2.9	81	6.7	70	4.0
HEAVY INDUSTRY	80	10.2	74	8.6	0.0	0.0	157	15.2	27	2.4	62	5.1	68	3.9
MACHINERY	70	8.9	0.0	0.0	0.0	0.0	0.0	0.0	0.0	0.0	1	0.1	53	3.0
CONSTRUCTION	0.0	0.0	0.0	0.0	0.0	0.0	0.0	0.0	0.0	0.0	0.0	0.0	221	12.6
ENERGY	0.0	0.0	107	12.5	107	11.4	214	20.8	0.0	0.0	251	20.7	279	15.9
TRADE	245	31.2	379	44.2	536	57.1	252	24.4	245	21.9	251	20.7	253	14.4
TRANSPORT	1	0.1	0.0	0.0	53	5.7	184	17.8	91	8.1	250	20.6	92	5.3
FINANCE	0.0	0.0	0.0	0.0	0.0	0.0	0.0	0.0	0.0	0.0	0.0	0.0	162	9.2
SERVICES	246	31.3	152	17.7	80	8.5	111	10.8	724	64.7	299	24.6	265	15.1
TOTAL	785	100.0	858	100.0	939	100.0	1030	100.0	1119	100.0	1213	100.0	1754	100.0

TABLE VIII.3 IMPORTS, EXPORTS, BALANCE OF TRADE, EXTERNAL DEBT
AUSTRALES OF 1970

SECTOR		YEAR 0	YEAR 1	YEAR 2	YEAR 3	YEAR 4	YEAR 5	YEAR 10
AGRICULTURE	IMPORTS	36	36	36	38	39	41	187
	EXPORTS	559	621	645	592	568	535	0.0
	B. T.	523	585	609	554	529	494	-187
FOOD PROCESSING	IMPORTS	5	5	5	83	224	362	8
	EXPORTS	463	220	4	0.0	0.0	0.0	173
	B. T.	458	215	-1	-83	-224	-362	166
LIGHT INDUSTRY	IMPORTS	802	480	247	225	254	277	376
	EXPORTS	22	22	23	122	351	340	104
	B. T.	-780	-458	-224	-103	97	62	-272
HEAVY INDUSTRY	IMPORTS	154	196	234	264	302	329	467
	EXPORTS	137	127	119	61	130	115	411
	B. T.	-17	-69	-115	-202	-172	-214	-56
MACHINERY	IMPORTS	847	444	167	140	144	155	199
	EXPORTS	17	17	18	18	243	250	93
	B. T.	-830	-426	-150	-122	99	95	-106
CONSTRUCTION	IMPORTS	39	37	62	0.0	25	0.0	0.0
	EXPORTS	0.0	0.0	0.0	150	0.0	128	9
	B. T.	-39	-37	-62	150	-25	128	9
ENERGY	IMPORTS	51	53	55	57	62	65	97
	EXPORTS	651	467	328	205	140	40	22
	B. T.	600	414	273	148	78	-25	-75
TRADE	IMPORTS	1781	1804	1648	1348	1135	918	12
	EXPORTS	0.0	0.0	0.0	0.0	0.0	0.0	31
	B. T.	-1781	-1804	-1648	-1348	-1135	-918	19
TRANSPORT	IMPORTS	36	38	39	40	43	44	196
	EXPORTS	878	786	667	534	436	344	0.0
	B. T.	842	748	627	493	393	299	-196
FINANCE	IMPORTS	7	9	11	13	15	17	26
	EXPORTS	655	695	721	735	742	742	751
	B. T.	648	686	709	722	727	725	725
SERVICES	IMPORTS	4	5	20	207	367	263	26
	EXPORTS	380	151	0.0	0.0	0.0	0.0	0.0
	B. T.	376	146	-20	-207	-367	-283	-26
TOTAL	IMPORTS	3763	3106	2524	2416	2610	2492	1593
	EXPORTS	3763	3106	2524	2416	2610	2492	1593
	B. T.	0.0	0.0	0.0	0.0	0.0	0.0	0.0
EXTERNAL DEBT		4800	5376	6022	6744	7553	8460	14909

TABLE VIII.4 INCOME BY INCOME GROUP
AUSTRALES OF 1970

INCOME GROUP	YEAR 0		YEAR 1		YEAR 2		YEAR 3		YEAR 4		YEAR 5		YEAR 10	
HIGH	4392	50.3	4677	49.0	5018	48.0	5390	47.0	5730	46.0	6074	45.0	7808	40.0
MIDDLE	3955	45.3	4295	45.0	4704	45.0	5275	46.0	5854	47.0	6479	48.0	10345	53.0
LOW	384	4.4	573	6.0	732	7.0	803	7.0	872	7.0	945	7.0	1366	7.0
TOTAL	8732	100.0	9545	100.0	10454	100.0	11468	100.0	12456	100.0	13499	100.0	19520	100.0

WELFARE INDICATORS	YEAR 0	YEAR 1	YEAR 2	YEAR 3	YEAR 4	YEAR 5	YEAR 10
NATIONAL INCOME	8732	9545	10454	11468	12456	13499	19520
DEMOCRATIC INDEX	0.787	0.830	0.850	0.858	0.868	0.870	0.925
POVERTY WEIGHTED	0.483	0.545	0.579	0.586	0.596	0.600	0.652
EFFICIENCY-EQUITY	4904	5636	6372	7057	7739	8470	12879
GINI	0.438	0.410	0.390	0.385	0.379	0.373	0.340

Simulation IX

TABLE IX.1 GROSS OUTPUTS
AUSTRALES OF 1970

SECTOR	YEAR 0	YEAR 1	YEAR 2	YEAR 3	YEAR 4	YEAR 5	YEAR 10	1/0	2/1	3/2	4/3	5/4	5/0	10/5	10/0
								ANNUAL GROWTH RATES (PERCENT)							
AGRICULTURE	1889	1943	1993	2044	2100	2159	2528	2.8	2.6	2.6	2.7	2.8	2.7	3.2	3.0
FOOD PROCESSING	2089	1971	1911	1880	1880	1908	2381	-5.6	-3.0	-1.7	0.0	1.5	-1.8	4.5	1.3
LIGHT INDUSTRY	1981	2519	2890	3214	3494	3729	4581	27.2	14.7	11.2	8.7	6.7	13.5	4.2	8.7
HEAVY INDUSTRY	660	699	733	769	806	846	1088	5.9	4.8	4.9	4.9	4.9	5.1	5.2	5.1
MACHINERY	894	1853	3509	5511	7737	10260	27623	107.2	89.4	57.1	40.4	32.6	62.9	21.9	40.9
CONSTRUCTION	735	929	1094	1247	1377	1493	1961	26.3	17.8	14.1	10.4	8.4	15.2	5.6	10.3
ENERGY	1651	1584	1534	1495	1469	1453	1485	-4.0	-3.2	-2.6	-1.7	-1.1	-2.5	0.4	-1.1
TRADE	1653	1802	1912	2011	2104	2189	2586	9.1	6.1	5.2	4.6	4.0	5.8	3.4	4.6
TRANSPORT	1898	1934	1951	1965	1981	1996	2075	1.9	0.9	0.7	0.8	0.7	1.0	0.8	0.9
FINANCE	963	1026	1094	1158	1220	1282	1616	6.5	6.5	5.9	5.3	5.0	5.9	4.7	5.3
SERVICES	2023	1922	1855	1803	1766	1744	1772	-5.0	-3.5	-2.8	-2.0	-1.3	-2.9	0.3	-1.3
TOTAL	16437	18182	20475	23097	25935	29057	49696	10.6	12.6	12.8	12.3	12.0	12.1	11.3	11.7

TABLE IX.1A GROSS OUTPUTS
AUSTRALES OF 1970

SECTOR	YEAR 0	YEAR 5	YEAR 6	YEAR 7	YEAR 8	YEAR 9	YEAR 10	6/5	7/6	8/7	9/8	10/9	5/0	10/5	10/0
								ANNUAL GROWTH RATES (PERCENT)							
AGRICULTURE	1889	2074	2113	2152	2192	2234	2277	1.8	1.9	1.9	1.9	1.9	1.9	1.9	1.9
FOOD PROCESSING	2089	1944	1976	2020	2073	2135	2204	1.6	2.2	2.7	3.0	3.3	-1.4	2.5	0.5
LIGHT INDUSTRY	1981	3204	3327	3430	3518	3595	3664	3.8	3.1	2.6	2.2	1.9	10.1	2.7	6.3
HEAVY INDUSTRY	660	786	811	837	864	891	919	3.2	3.2	3.2	3.1	3.1	3.6	3.2	3.4
MACHINERY	894	7636	9409	11270	13214	15235	17329	23.2	19.8	17.2	15.3	13.7	53.6	17.8	34.5
CONSTRUCTION	735	1295	1362	1420	1471	1518	1562	5.2	4.2	3.6	3.2	2.9	12.0	3.8	7.8
ENERGY	1651	1498	1493	1493	1497	1504	1513	-0.4	0.0	0.3	0.5	0.6	-1.9	0.2	-0.9
TRADE	1653	2024	2073	2117	2160	2200	2240	2.4	2.2	2.0	1.9	1.8	4.1	2.0	3.1
TRANSPORT	1898	1955	1962	1970	1978	1986	1994	0.4	0.4	0.4	0.4	0.4	0.6	0.4	0.5
FINANCE	963	1199	1238	1276	1313	1350	1387	3.3	3.1	2.9	2.8	2.7	4.5	3.0	3.7
SERVICES	2023	1819	1811	1811	1815	1823	1834	-0.4	0.0	0.2	0.4	0.6	-2.1	0.2	-1.0
TOTAL	16437	25434	27576	29796	32095	34471	36921	8.4	8.1	7.7	7.4	7.1	9.1	7.7	8.4

TABLE IX.2 PUBLIC INVESTMENT BY DESTINATION
AUSTRALES OF 1970

SECTOR	YEAR 0		YEAR 1		YEAR 2		YEAR 3		YEAR 4		YEAR 5		YEAR 10	
AGRICULTURE	16	3.0	18	3.0	19	3.0	21	3.0	23	3.0	25	3.0	40	3.0
FOOD PROCESSING	16	3.0	18	3.0	19	3.0	21	3.0	23	3.0	25	3.0	40	3.0
LIGHT INDUSTRY	16	3.0	18	3.0	19	3.0	21	3.0	23	3.0	25	3.0	40	3.0
HEAVY INDUSTRY	16	3.0	18	3.0	19	3.0	21	3.0	23	3.0	25	3.0	40	3.0
MACHINERY	381	70.0	412	70.0	453	70.0	496	70.0	542	70.0	593	70.0	936	70.0
CONSTRUCTION	16	3.0	18	3.0	19	3.0	21	3.0	23	3.0	25	3.0	40	3.0
ENERGY	16	3.0	18	3.0	19	3.0	21	3.0	23	3.0	25	3.0	40	3.0
TRADE	16	3.0	18	3.0	19	3.0	21	3.0	23	3.0	25	3.0	40	3.0
TRANSPORT	16	3.0	18	3.0	19	3.0	21	3.0	23	3.0	25	3.0	40	3.0
FINANCE	16	3.0	18	3.0	19	3.0	21	3.0	23	3.0	25	3.0	40	3.0
SERVICES	16	3.0	18	3.0	19	3.0	21	3.0	23	3.0	25	3.0	41	3.0
TOTAL	544	100.0	589	100.0	647	100.0	708	100.0	774	100.0	847	100.0	1337	100.0

TABLE IX.3 IMPORTS, EXPORTS, BALANCE OF TRADE, EXTERNAL DEBT

AUSTRALES OF 1970

SECTOR		YEAR 0	YEAR 1	YEAR 2	YEAR 3	YEAR 4	YEAR 5	YEAR 10
AGRICULTURE	IMPORTS	36	36	36	36	37	38	46
	EXPORTS	560	617	648	668	678	679	574
	B. T.	524	582	612	632	641	641	528
FOOD PROCESSING	IMPORTS	5	5	5	45	175	291	793
	EXPORTS	463	268	109	0.0	0.0	0.0	0.0
	B. T.	458	263	104	-45	-175	-291	-793
LIGHT INDUSTRY	IMPORTS	790	672	717	832	1002	1235	3264
	EXPORTS	22	22	23	23	24	24	27
	B. T.	-768	-650	-694	-809	-978	-1211	-3237
HEAVY INDUSTRY	IMPORTS	154	195	369	627	898	1200	3252
	EXPORTS	154	72	30	31	31	32	35
	B. T.	0.0	-124	-339	-596	-867	-1168	-3217
MACHINERY	IMPORTS	596	121	214	326	450	592	1561
	EXPORTS	17	256	1600	3271	5122	7219	21725
	B. T.	-579	136	1386	2945	4671	6627	20164
CONSTRUCTION	IMPORTS	0.0	0.0	0.0	0.0	0.0	0.0	0.0
	EXPORTS	332	475	592	700	781	843	976
	B. T.	332	475	592	700	781	843	976
ENERGY	IMPORTS	51	52	52	53	54	86	813
	EXPORTS	651	519	386	250	119	20	22
	B. T.	600	467	334	197	65	-66	-791
TRADE	IMPORTS	1781	2007	2404	2917	3491	4142	8658
	EXPORTS	0.0	0.0	0.0	0.0	0.0	0.0	0.0
	B. T.	-1781	-2007	-2404	-2917	-3491	-4142	-8658
TRANSPORT	IMPORTS	36	37	38	38	39	40	1492
	EXPORTS	878	782	627	443	245	24	0.0
	B. T.	842	745	589	405	206	-15	-1492
FINANCE	IMPORTS	7	10	13	17	21	26	57
	EXPORTS	655	689	722	751	776	798	894
	B. T.	648	679	709	734	755	772	837
SERVICES	IMPORTS	4	4	119	396	676	965	2678
	EXPORTS	380	142	0.0	0.0	0.0	0.0	0.0
	B. T.	376	138	-119	-396	-676	-965	-2678
TOTAL	IMPORTS	3461	3138	3966	5287	6843	8614	22616
	EXPORTS	4113	3842	4737	6136	7776	9639	24253
	B. T.	652	704	771	849	932	1025	1637
EXTERNAL DEBT		4148	3942	3643	3232	2687	1985	-5024

TABLE IX.4 SECTORAL EMPLOYMENT

EMPLOYED PERSONS

SECTOR	YEAR 0		YEAR 1		YEAR 2		YEAR 3		YEAR 4		YEAR 5		YEAR 10	
AGRICULTURE	1338116	16.1	1360179	15.5	1379155	14.9	1398487	14.3	1420050	13.8	1442983	13.3	1594315	11.2
FOOD PROCESSING	349638	4.2	326178	3.7	312633	3.4	303913	3.4	300435	2.9	301374	2.8	354991	2.5
LIGHT INDUSTRY	669483	8.0	841446	9.6	954393	10.3	1049214	10.8	1127309	11.0	1189508	11.0	1378890	9.7
HEAVY INDUSTRY	502784	6.0	526454	6.0	545328	5.9	565283	5.8	586157	5.7	607651	5.6	737696	5.2
MACHINERY	148982	1.8	305115	3.5	571137	6.2	886683	9.1	1230584	12.0	1613014	14.9	4097998	28.8
CONSTRUCTION	513584	6.2	641207	7.3	746328	8.1	841446	8.6	918431	8.9	983826	9.1	1219698	8.6
ENERGY	166767	2.0	158172	1.8	151405	1.6	145818	1.5	141626	1.4	138485	1.3	133552	0.9
TRADE	1303793	15.7	1405440	16.0	1473999	16.0	1532417	15.7	1584538	15.4	1629462	15.0	1816909	12.8
TRANSPORT	443987	5.3	447144	5.1	445886	4.8	443879	4.6	442333	4.3	440506	4.1	432230	3.0
FINANCE	303562	3.6	319708	3.6	336667	3.6	352525	3.6	367096	3.6	381133	3.5	453306	3.2
SERVICES	2589991	31.1	2431995	27.8	2320073	25.1	2228889	22.9	2158552	21.0	2106172	19.4	2019568	14.2
TOTAL	8330688	100.0	8763036	100.0	9237005	100.0	9748554	100.0	10277114	100.0	10834115	100.0	14239154	100.0

TABLE IX.5 INCOME BY INCOME GROUP

AUSTRALES OF 1970

INCOME GROUP	YEAR 0		YEAR 1		YEAR 2		YEAR 3		YEAR 4		YEAR 5		YEAR 10	
HIGH	4392	50.3	4616	49.0	4955	48.0	5338	47.0	5741	46.0	6173	45.0	8765	40.0
MIDDLE	3955	45.3	4239	45.0	4646	45.0	5224	46.0	5866	47.0	6584	48.0	11614	53.0
LOW	384	4.4	565	6.0	723	7.0	795	7.0	874	7.0	960	7.0	1534	7.0
TOTAL	8732	100.0	9420	100.0	10324	100.0	11357	100.0	12480	100.0	13717	100.0	21913	100.0

WELFARE INDICATORS	YEAR 0	YEAR 1	YEAR 2	YEAR 3	YEAR 4	YEAR 5	YEAR 10
NATIONAL INCOME	8732	9420	10324	11357	12480	13717	21913
DEMOCRATIC INDEX	0.787	0.851	0.908	0.955	1.004	1.056	1.330
POVERTY WEIGHTED	0.483	0.559	0.618	0.653	0.689	0.728	0.939
EFFICIENCY-EQUITY	4904	5562	6292	6989	7754	8607	14458
GINI	0.438	0.410	0.390	0.385	0.379	0.373	0.340

Simulation X

TABLE X.1 GROSS OUTPUTS
AUSTRALES OF 1970

SECTOR	YEAR 0	YEAR 1	YEAR 2	YEAR 3	YEAR 4	YEAR 5	YEAR 10
AGRICULTURE	1889	2127	2537	3009	3434	3943	6936
FOOD PROCESSING	2089	2013	2044	2124	2248	2413	3653
LIGHT INDUSTRY	1981	2534	2933	3285	3590	3852	4851
HEAVY INDUSTRY	660	708	760	818	880	946	1338
MACHINERY	894	1160	1373	1572	1757	1927	2685
CONSTRUCTION	735	925	1080	1220	1334	1430	1771
ENERGY	1651	1588	1546	1519	1506	1506	1622
TRADE	1653	1835	2010	2185	2418	2613	3576
TRANSPORT	1898	1932	1946	1957	1969	1979	2033
FINANCE	963	1055	1181	1315	1452	1595	2394
SERVICES	2023	1929	1878	1847	1834	1839	2016
TOTAL	16437	17806	19287	20851	22423	24044	32874

ANNUAL GROWTH RATES (PERCENT)

SECTOR	1/0	2/1	3/2	4/3	5/4	5/0	10/5	10/0
AGRICULTURE	12.6	19.3	18.6	14.1	14.8	15.9	12.0	13.9
FOOD PROCESSING	-3.6	1.5	3.9	5.8	7.3	2.9	8.7	5.8
LIGHT INDUSTRY	27.9	15.8	12.0	9.3	7.3	14.2	4.7	9.4
HEAVY INDUSTRY	7.2	7.4	7.6	7.6	7.5	7.5	7.2	7.3
MACHINERY	29.7	18.3	14.5	11.8	9.7	16.6	6.9	11.6
CONSTRUCTION	25.8	16.8	13.0	9.3	7.2	14.2	4.4	9.2
ENERGY	-3.8	-2.6	-1.8	-0.8	0.0	-1.8	1.5	-0.2
TRADE	11.0	9.5	8.7	10.6	8.1	9.6	6.5	8.0
TRANSPORT	1.8	0.7	0.5	0.6	0.5	0.8	0.5	0.7
FINANCE	9.5	11.9	11.4	10.4	9.9	10.6	8.5	9.5
SERVICES	-4.7	-2.7	-1.6	-0.7	0.2	-1.9	1.9	0.0
TOTAL	8.3	8.3	8.1	7.5	7.2	7.9	6.5	7.2

TABLE X.2 PUBLIC INVESTMENT BY DESTINATION
AUSTRALES OF 1970

SECTOR	YEAR 0		YEAR 1		YEAR 2		YEAR 3		YEAR 4		YEAR 5		YEAR 10	
AGRICULTURE	223	40.9	220	37.7	229	36.6	153	22.9	246	34.9	260	34.7	318	32.7
FOOD PROCESSING	41	7.6	44	7.9	50	7.9	54	8.2	58	8.2	61	8.2	82	8.4
LIGHT INDUSTRY	33	6.0	38	6.6	42	6.8	45	6.8	48	6.9	52	6.9	70	7.2
HEAVY INDUSTRY	31	5.7	36	6.2	39	6.3	43	6.5	46	6.5	49	6.6	67	6.9
MACHINERY	21	3.8	20	3.5	21	3.4	22	3.3	23	3.2	24	3.2	29	3.0
CONSTRUCTION	10	1.9	13	2.3	15	2.4	18	2.7	19	2.7	21	2.8	29	3.0
ENERGY	27	4.9	31	5.4	35	5.5	38	5.7	41	5.8	44	5.9	60	6.2
TRADE	62	11.4	66	11.4	72	11.5	158	23.8	81	11.5	86	11.5	112	11.5
TRANSPORT	6	1.1	10	1.8	13	2.1	15	2.3	17	2.5	19	2.5	29	3.0
FINANCE	57	10.4	62	10.6	66	10.6	71	10.7	76	10.7	80	10.7	105	10.8
SERVICES	34	6.3	39	6.7	43	6.9	47	7.0	50	7.1	53	7.1	71	7.3
TOTAL	544	100.0	582	100.0	625	100.0	666	100.0	706	100.0	748	100.0	973	100.0

TABLE X.3 IMPORTS, EXPORTS, BALANCE OF TRADE, EXTERNAL DEBT
AUSTRALES OF 1970

SECTOR		YEAR 0	YEAR 1	YEAR 2	YEAR 3	YEAR 4	YEAR 5	YEAR 10
AGRICULTURE	IMPORTS	36	37	38	41	44	47	70
	EXPORTS	554	766	1104	1486	1801	2181	4336
	B. T.	518	730	1066	1445	1757	2133	4266
FOOD PROCESSING	IMPORTS	5	5	5	5	6	6	8
	EXPORTS	463	306	232	191	188	214	642
	B. T.	458	301	226	185	182	208	634
LIGHT INDUSTRY	IMPORTS	798	627	550	489	496	520	901
	EXPORTS	22	22	23	23	24	24	27
	B. T.	-776	-605	-527	-466	-472	-496	-874
HEAVY INDUSTRY	IMPORTS	154	180	201	222	242	262	358
	EXPORTS	157	143	124	106	103	107	207
	B. T.	2	-37	-77	-116	-139	-155	-151
MACHINERY	IMPORTS	524	296	175	107	118	129	175
	EXPORTS	17	17	18	98	207	308	664
	B. T.	-507	-278	-158	-9	89	179	489
CONSTRUCTION	IMPORTS	0.0	0.0	0.0	0.0	0.0	0.0	0.0
	EXPORTS	272	354	449	504	602	662	833
	B. T.	272	354	449	504	602	662	833
ENERGY	IMPORTS	51	52	53	54	56	57	259
	EXPORTS	651	530	423	322	233	154	22
	B. T.	600	477	370	267	177	96	-237
TRADE	IMPORTS	1781	1897	2060	2274	2428	2639	3937
	EXPORTS	0.0	0.0	0.0	0.0	0.0	0.0	0.0
	B. T.	-1781	-1897	-2060	-2274	-2428	-2639	-3937
TRANSPORT	IMPORTS	36	37	38	39	40	41	210
	EXPORTS	878	811	719	617	516	410	0.0
	B. T.	842	774	681	578	476	370	-210
FINANCE	IMPORTS	7	9	9	10	11	12	16
	EXPORTS	655	716	806	902	1000	1103	1682
	B. T.	648	708	796	892	988	1090	1665
SERVICES	IMPORTS	4	4	18	203	372	530	1231
	EXPORTS	380	173	0.0	0.0	0.0	0.0	0.0
	B. T.	376	169	-18	-203	-372	-530	-1231
TOTAL	IMPORTS	3398	3143	3148	3445	3813	4243	7166
	EXPORTS	4050	3839	3896	4248	4673	5162	8412
	B. T.	652	697	748	803	860	919	1246
EXTERNAL DEBT		4148	3949	3675	3312	2850	2273	-2958

TABLE X.4 SECTORAL EMPLOYMENT
EMPLOYED PERSONS

SECTOR	YEAR 0		YEAR 1		YEAR 2		YEAR 3		YEAR 4		YEAR 5		YEAR 10	
AGRICULTURE	1338116	16.1	1489228	16.9	1755671	18.6	2058648	20.4	2322223	21.6	2635200	23.1	4374631	29.5
FOOD PROCESSING	349638	4.2	333165	3.8	334331	3.5	343399	3.4	359276	3.3	381101	3.3	544565	3.7
LIGHT INDUSTRY	669483	8.0	846482	9.6	968556	10.3	1072396	10.6	1158429	10.8	1228528	10.8	1460134	9.8
HEAVY INDUSTRY	502784	6.0	532830	6.0	565396	6.0	601575	6.0	640009	6.0	680214	6.0	907108	6.1
MACHINERY	148982	1.8	191055	2.2	223442	2.4	252928	2.5	279414	2.6	303022	2.7	398378	2.7
CONSTRUCTION	513584	6.2	638410	7.2	737293	7.8	823277	8.2	889693	8.3	942832	8.3	1101675	7.4
ENERGY	166767	2.0	158508	1.8	152580	1.6	148132	1.5	145244	1.4	143544	1.3	145897	1.0
TRADE	1303793	15.7	1430852	16.2	1549139	16.4	1664999	16.5	1820769	17.0	1945331	17.1	2511781	16.9
TRANSPORT	443987	5.3	446738	5.1	444765	4.7	441975	4.4	439593	4.1	436883	3.8	423382	2.9
FINANCE	303562	3.6	328667	3.7	363594	3.9	400279	4.0	436833	4.1	474344	4.2	671642	4.5
SERVICES	2589991	31.1	2440545	27.6	2348386	24.9	2283083	22.6	2241832	20.9	2221168	19.5	2297986	15.5
TOTAL	8330688	100.0	8836480	100.0	9443154	100.0	10090690	100.0	10733315	100.0	11392168	100.0	14837178	100.0

TABLE X.5 INCOME BY INCOME GROUP
AUSTRALES OF 1970

INCOME GROUP	YEAR 0		YEAR 1		YEAR 2		YEAR 3		YEAR 4		YEAR 5		YEAR 10	
HIGH	4392	50.3	4569	49.0	4806	48.0	5053	47.0	5295	46.0	5535	45.0	6673	40.0
MIDDLE	3955	45.3	4196	45.0	4505	45.0	4946	46.0	5410	47.0	5904	48.0	8841	53.0
LOW	384	4.4	559	6.0	701	7.0	753	7.0	806	7.0	861	7.0	1168	7.0
TOTAL	8732	100.0	9324	100.0	10012	100.0	10752	100.0	11510	100.0	12300	100.0	16682	100.0

WELFARE INDICATORS	YEAR 0	YEAR 1	YEAR 2	YEAR 3	YEAR 4	YEAR 5	YEAR 10
NATIONAL INCOME	8732	9324	10012	10752	11510	12300	16682
DEMOCRATIC INDEX	0.787	0.835	0.862	0.874	0.887	0.900	0.972
POVERTY WEIGHTED	0.483	0.549	0.586	0.597	0.609	0.621	0.686
EFFICIENCY-EQUITY	4904	5506	6102	6617	7152	7718	11007
GINI	0.438	0.410	0.390	0.385	0.379	0.373	0.340

References

Abadie, J. (1978), 'The GRG Method for Nonlinear Programming', in Greenberg (1978).

Abadie, J. and J.Carpentier (1965), 'Généralisation de la méthode du gradient réduit de Wolfe au cas de contraintes non-linéaires', Note HR6678, Electricité de France, Paris.

ACIJ (Agencia de Cooperación Internacional del Japón) (1987), *Estudio sobre el Desarrollo Económico de la República Argentina. Informe final.*

Aglietta, M. (1985), 'Europe: La décennie tous les dangers', *Seminario sobre Crisis y Regulación Estatal,* EURAL (Instituto de Investigaciones Europeo-Latinoamericanas), Buenos Aires.

Argentina (1975), *Sistema de Cuentas del Producto e Ingreso de la Argentina,* Banco Central de la República Argentina.

Argentina (1977), *Censo Nacional de 1970,* Dirección Nacional de Estadística y Censos.

Argentina (1983), *Censo Nacional de Población y Vivienda 1980,* Instituto Nacional de Estadística y Censos.

Argentina (1985a), *Lineamientos de una Estrategia de Crecimiento Económico, 1985-1989,* Presidencia de la Nación, Secretaría de Planificación.

Argentina (1985b), *Estimaciones Trimestrales sobre Oferta y Demanda Global,* Banco Central de la República Argentina.

Argentina (1986a), *Estimaciones Trimestrales de Oferta y Demanda Global,* Banco Central de la República Argentina.

Argentina (1986b), *Proyección de Población 1970-2025,* Instituto Nacional de Estadística y Censos.

Argentina (1986c), *Cuadro de Insumo-Producto de los Sectores Productores de Bienes. Argentina 1973.* Versión Preliminar. Secretaría de Planificación de la Presidencia de la Nación - Banco Central de la República Argentina.

Argentina (1987), *Encuesta Permanente de Hogares: Presentación de Datos del Gran Buenos Aires - Abril 1987.* Instituto Nacional de Estadística y Censos.

Azpiazu, D., R. Bisang, B. Kosakoff (1988), 'Industrialización y exportación de manufacturas en la Argentina. Evolución estructural y apertura exportadora (1973-1986)', *Boletín Informativo Techint* (253), 25-76.

Batra, R. (1985), *The Great Depression of 1990,* Venus Books, Dallas.

Blejer, M.I. and A. Cheasty (1986), 'Using Fiscal Measures to Stimulate Savings in Developing Countries', *Finance and Development* 23(2), 16-19.

Blitzer, C., P.B. Clark and L. Taylor, eds (1975), *Economy-Wide Models and Development Planning*, Oxford University Press, London.

Blumenthal, W.M. (1988), 'The World Economy and Technological Change', *Foreign Affairs* 66(3), 529-50.

Boyer, R., comp. (1986), *Capitalismes fin de siècle*, Presses Universitaires de France, Paris.

Brandt, W. et al. (1980), *North-South: A Programme for Survival*, Pan Books, London.

Brandt, W. et al. (1983), *Common Crisis,* Pan Books, London.

Buzaglo, J. (1984), *Planning the Mexican Economy: Alternative Development Strategies*, Croom Helm, London; St.Martins Press, New York.

Calleo, D.P., H.v.B.Cleveland and L.Silk (1988), 'The Dollar and the Defense of the West', *Foreign Affairs* 66(4), 846-862.

Canavese, A. (1982), 'The Structuralist Explanation in the Theory of Inflation', *World Development* 10, 523-29.

CEPAL (Comisión Económica para América Latina y el Caribe) (1986), *La distribución personal del ingreso en el Gran Buenos Aires en el período 1974-1983,* Documento de Trabajo No.23, Buenos Aires.

Clark, P.B. (1975), 'Intersectoral Consistency and Macroeconomic Planning', in Blitzer, Clark and Taylor (1975).

Conesa, E. (1986), *Fuga de Capitales*, Instituto de Política Económica y Social, Buenos Aires.

Costa, A.M. (1983), 'DYNAMICO: A multilevel programming model of world trade and development', in B.G. Hickman (ed), *Global International Economic Models,* North-Holland, Amsterdam.

Crockett, A. (1988), 'Indicators and International Economic Cooperation', *Finance and Development* 25(3), 20-24.

Cuddington, J.T. (1986), *Capital Flight: Estimates, Issues, and Explanations,* Princeton Studies in International Finance No. 58, Department of Economics, Princeton University.

Cumby R. and R. Levich (1987), 'On the Definition and Magnitude of Recent Capital Flight', in Lessard and Williamson (1987).

Chenery, H.B., M.S. Ahluwalia, C.L.G. Bell, J.H. Duloy and R. Jolly (1974), *Redistribution with Growth*, Oxford University Press, Oxford.

Chenery, H.B. and M. Syrquin (1975), *Patterns of Development, 1950-1970*, Oxford University Press, London.

Dell, S., ed. (1987), *The International Monetary System and its Reform,* North-Holland, Amsterdam.

Dervis, K., J. de Melo and S. Robinson (1982), *General equilibrium models for development policy*, Cambridge University Press, Cambridge.

Díaz Alejandro, C. (1983), 'Stories of the 1930s in the 1980s', in P. Aspe Armella, R. Dornbusch and M. Obstfeld, eds, 1983, *Financial Policies and the World Capital Market: The Problem of the Latin American Countries,* University of Chicago Press, Chicago.

Di Matteo, M. and R.M. Goodwin, eds., (1989), *Technological and social factors in long term fluctuations*, Springer, New York.

Dooley, M., W.Helkie, R.Tyron, and J.Underwood (1986), 'An Analysis of External Debt Positions of Eight Developing Countries through 1990', *Journal of Development Economics* 21, 283-318.

Elmandjra, M. (1988), 'UN Organizations: Ways to their Reactivation', *ifda dossier* (67), 45-50.

Ferencz, B.B. and K. Keyes (1988), *PlanetHood*, Vision Books, Coos Bay.

Ferrer, A. (1987), 'El Sistema Centro-Periferia y la Política Económica. Una Ilustración sobre el Caso Argentino', *Pensamiento Iberoamericano* 11, 59-82.

Fields, G.S. (1989), 'Changes in Poverty and Inequality in Developing Countries', *The World Bank Research Observer* 4(2), 167-85.

Foster, J. (1987), *Evolutionary Macroeconomics*, Allen and Unwin, London.

Gill, M. (1988), 'Statisticians Consider Ways to Reduce Current Account Discrepancy', *IMF Survey* 17(11), 165-6.

Goodwin, R.M. (1986), 'Swinging along the turnpike with von Neumann and Sraffa', *Cambridge Journal of Economics* 10, 203-210.

Goodwin, R.M. and L.F.Punzo (1987), *The Dynamics of a Capitalist Economy: A Multisectoral Approach*, Polity Press, Cambridge; Basil Blackwell, Oxford.

Granberg, A. and A. Rubinshtein (1984), 'Some lines on development of the United Nations global input-output model', *Proceedings of the Seventh International Conference on Input-Output Techniques,* United Nations, New York.

Greenberg, H.J., ed. (1978), *Design and implementation of optimization software,* Sijthoff & Noordhoff, Alphen aan den Rijn.

Gulati, S.K. (1987), 'A Note on Trade Misinvoicing', in Lessard and Williamson (1987).

Guth, W. (1988), *Economic Policy Coordination*, International Monetary Fund, Washington.

ISML (1984), *Fortran Subrutines for Mathematics and Statistics,* ISML, Houston.

Kaldor, N. (1983), 'The role of commodity prices in economic recovery', *Lloyd's Bank Review* (July). Reprinted in F. Targetti and A.P. Thirlwall (eds) (1989), *The Essential Kaldor,* Duckworth, London.

Kalecki, M. (1960), 'Unemployment in Underdeveloped Countries', *Indian Journal of Labour Economics* III (2), 59-61. Reprinted in M. Kalecki (1976), *Essays on Developing Economies,* The Harvester Press, Hassocks.

Kaplinsky, R. (1989), ' "Technological Revolution" and the International Division of Labour in Manufacturing: A Place for the Third World?', in R. Kaplinsky and C. Cooper (eds), *Technology and Development in the Third Industrial Revolution,* Frank Cass, London.

Khan, M.S. and N. Ul Haque (1987), 'Capital Flight from Developing Countries', *Finance & Development* 24(1), 2-5.

Lasdon, L.S. and A.D. Waren (1978), 'Generalized Reduced Gradient Software for Linearly and Nonlinearly Constrained Problems', in Greenberg (1978).

Lasdon, L.S., A.D. Waren and M.W. Ratner (1980), *GRG2 User's Guide*, University of Texas, Austin.

Lee, T.H. and P.P. Reid , eds (1991), *National Interests in an Age of Global Technology*, National Academy Press, Washington.

Leff, N.H. and K. Sato (1987), 'The Prospects for Higher Domestic Saving Rates in Latin America', *Journal of Policy Modeling* 9(4), 559-576.

Leontief, W. and F. Duchin (1983), *Military Spending,* Oxford University Press, New York.

Lessard, D.R. and J. Williamson, eds (1987), *Capital Flight and Third World Debt*, Institute for International Economics, Washington.

Liebman, J., L.S. Lasdon, L. Schrage and A. Waren (1986), *Modeling and Optimization with GINO*, Scientific Press, Palo Alto.

Lifschitz, E. and P. Liachovitzky, with the collaboration of R. Natalucci (1986), *Matriz de Importaciones de Bienes de Capital 1983,* Versión Provisoria, Documento de trabajo No 4, Secretaría de Planificación, Buenos Aires.

Llach, J.J. (1988), 'Estructura y dinámica del empleo en la Argentina: diagnóstico y perspectivas', *Boletín Informativo Techint* (251), 79-103.

Lluch, C. (1973), 'The Extended Linear Expenditure System', *European Economic Review* 4, 21-32.

Marquardt, D.W. (1963), 'An algorithm for least-squares estimation of non-linear parameters', *Journal of the Society for Industrial and Applied Mathematics* 11(2), 431-41.

Marris, S. (1987), *Deficits and the Dollar: The World Economy at Risk,* Institute for International Economics, Washington.

Meidner, R. (1978), *Employee Investment Funds: An Approach to Collective Capital Formation,* Allen and Unwin, London.

Mistral, J. (1986), 'Régime international et trajectoires nationales', in Boyer (1986).

Morgan Guaranty Trust (1986), 'LDC Capital Flight', *World Financial Markets* (March), 13-15.

Nikaido, H. (1975), *Monopolistic Competition and Effective Demand,* Princeton University Press, Princeton.

OECD (Organisation for Economic Co-operation and Development) (1988), *Historical Statistics 1960-1986,* Paris.

OECD (Organisation for Economic Co-operation and Development) (1991), *Main Economic Indicators.* Paris.

Pyatt, G. and J.I. Round (1985), *Social Accounting Matrices - A Basis for Planning,* The World Bank, Washington D.C.

Pyatt, G. and E. Thorbecke (1976), *Planning Techniques for a Better Future,* International Labour Office, Geneva.

Rosenthal, G. (1991), 'Balance preliminar de la economía de América Latina y el Caribe, 1990', *Comercio Exterior* 41(3), 281-303.

Royer, J. (1986), 'The Long-Term Employment Impact of Disarmament Policies', Working Paper No.3, Disarmament and Employment Programme, International Labour Office, Geneva.

Scott, M.F.G. (1989), *A New View of Economic Growth,* Oxford University Press, New York.

Sen, A. (1979), 'The Welfare Basis of Real Income Comparisons: A Survey', *Journal of Economic Literature* 1, 1-45.

SIPRI (Stockholm International Peace Research Institute) (1984), *Sipri Yearbook 1984,* Frances and Pinter, London.

SIPRI (Stockholm International Peace Research Institute) (1986), *Sipri Yearbook 1986,* Oxford University Press, Oxford.

South Commission (1990), *The Challenge to the South,* Oxford University Press, Oxford.

Sraffa, P. (1960), *Production of Commodities by Means of Commodities,* Cambridge University Press, Cambridge.

Stone, R. (1954), 'Linear Expenditure Systems and Demand Analysis, An Application to the Pattern of British Demand', *Economic Journal* 255, 511-527.

Streeten, P. (1991), 'Global Prospects in an Interdependent World', *World Development* 19(1), 123-133.

Taylor, L. (1975), 'Theoretical Foundations and Technical Implications', in Blitzer, Clark and Taylor (1975).

Thorbecke, E. (1985), 'The Social Accounting Matrix and Consistency-Type Planning Models', in G.Pyatt and J.I.Round, eds, *Social Accounting Matrices: A Basis for Planning,* The World Bank, Washington.

Thurow, L.C. (1985), 'Budget Deficits', in L.C.Thurow and D.Bell, *The Deficits: How Big? How Long? How Dangerous?*, New York University Press, New York.
Thurow, L.C. and L. D'Andrea Tyson (1987), 'The Economic Black Hole', *Foreign Policy* 67, 3-21.
Tinbergen, J. and D. Fischer (1987), *Warfare and Welfare: Integrating Security Policy into Socio-Economic Policy,* Wheatsheaf, Sussex; St. Martin's Press, New York.
Tokman, V. (1985), 'El proceso de acumulación y la debilidad de los actores', *Revista de la Cepal* 31, 219-243.
UN (United Nations) (1989), *World Economic Survey 1989,* New York.
UN (United Nations) (1990), *World Economic Survey 1990,* New York.
UNCTAD (United Nations Conference on Trade and Development) (1987), *Trade and Development Report, 1987,* Geneva.
Vines, D., J. Maciejowsky and J.E. Meade (1983), *Stagflation: Demand Management*, Allen and Unwin, London.
Weitzman, M.L. (1984), *The Share Economy: Conquering Stagflation,* Harvard University Press, Cambridge, Mass.
World Bank (1985), *Argentina Economic Memorandum: Main Report,* Washington.
World Bank (1987), *World Development Report 1987*, Oxford University Press, Washington.
World Bank (1988), *World Development Report 1988,* Oxford University Press, Washington.
World Bank (1989), *World Development Report 1989*, Oxford University Press, Washington.
World Bank (1990), *World Development Report 1990,* Oxford University Press, Washington.
World Bank (1991), *World Development Report 1991,* Oxford University Press, Washington.

For Product Safety Concerns and Information please contact our
EU representative GPSR@taylorandfrancis.com Taylor & Francis
Verlag GmbH, Kaufingerstraße 24, 80331 München, Germany